OLD TIMES

IN

ASSAM

OLD TIMES

IN

ASSAM.

BY

T. KINNEY.

GYAN

Published by

Gyan Publishing House
5, Ansari Road
Daryaganj, New Delhi-110002
Phone: 011-47034999, 9811692060
E-mail: books@gyanbooks.com

Distribution Network
gyanbooks.com
India, USA, Canada, UK, Australia, France

ISBN: 978-81-212-7206-3 (PB)
First Published, 1896

2nd Impression 2023

Printed at: Gyan Press, Delhi.

OLD TIMES IN ASSAM
Author: T. KINNEY

OLD TIMES

IN

ASSAM.

BY

J. KINNEY.

Calcutta:
PRINTED AND PUBLISHED AT THE "STAR" PRESS
19, LALL BAZAR STREET.

1896.

PREFACE.

The following pages contain nothing new or original. They are merely reprints from the columns of the *Englishman* and the *Indian Planters' Gazette*, and I have to thank the proprietors of those papers for permission to republish sketches of "old times" in Assam, which may prove interesting to a new generation of planters who know only the Assam of the present day, with its daily mail steamers on the river, and its improved communications and higher civilisation generally. There was much of interest in those old times which has never been recorded, and I can only hope that a more capable chronicler among the survivors of the early days of tea in Assam may be stirred up to fittingly record, for the admiration of the present generation, what was done and suffered by the pioneers of the tea industry in the Assam Valley and elsewhere.

T. Kinney.

CONTENTS.

THE EARLY "SIXTIES."

THE DIARY OF PEKOE TIPS.

I.—INTRODUCTORY.

TEZBRUSAUGAR is a tea district in India whose geographical position there is no necessity to describe. Every school boy ought to know where Tezbrusaugar is. The mighty waters of the Brahmaputra, from their distant sources near the Mansarowar Lake, roll down their golden sands through Hundes and Thibet; penetrate through an unexplored belt of mountains inhabited by unknown wild and savage tribes, reputed cannibals, whom even the known savages on the borders,—the Abors and Mishmis,—look on with fear; flow on through an exhuberantly fertile, not to say jungly valley; and eventually merge in the mighty ocean through the many mouths of the Ganges, or the Sanderbands.

Geographers are still somewhat uncertain on the subject of the connection between the Tsanpo of Thibet and the Brahmaputra, and undecided as to which is the right end of the former river. But the general public will at once be able to determine the geographical position of Tezbrusaugar from my description of the course of the Brahmaputra, when I add that the district is on both banks of the river, somewhere between Mansarowar and Mandalay. If that is still too indefinite, I may add it lies—but stay! perhaps I had better leave it there. It is as well not to be too particular in geographical description; the inhabitants might feel hurt.

Still less necessary is a local, or even a social description of the place where poor old Pekoe Tips lived and died.

But on second thoughts, as the tendency of the age is realistic, perhaps I had better add a few particulars.

Tezbrusaugar, as before remarked, is a tea district. It comprises some thousands of square miles in area; it has dozens of tea companies, scores of tea estates, and hundreds of tea gardens within its limits. It is situated, as before noted, on the banks of the Brahmaputra between (to be particular) Calcutta and China. It lies on both banks of the river: so do the inhabitants. It is governed by a Chief Commissioner, and more immediately by several Deputy Commissioners under him. It now, under our present enlightened *regime*, rejoices in numerous evidences of a high civilization, such as local boards, municipal committees, a Public Works Department, two distinct bodies of police, numerous gaols, several lunatic asylums, two inland steam navigation companies, and a railway. It exports a large quantity of tea, some children, and a few curious cases of malarial fever. It imports a lot of machinery; a good many bags of rice, and of crushed food for horses and cattle; a number of curious and expensive animals known as Act I. coolies; a considerable quantity of beer, lawn tennis materials, whisky, and Peliti's sweetmeats; and finally, a number of "young men from the country."

These young men "come out to tea." They are evidently misguided youths; for the classical poet observes (*vide* Mus: Hall Lit; Cap. VII. p. 199, *edition de luxe*)—

> "That good young man—that man called Dan
> "He always *came home to tea!*"

Hence it may be argued that it is a mistake to come out to tea. Far better go home to it.

It is the views and opinions of one of these misguided young men from the country, who, instead of going home—or staying at home—to tea, was weak enough to come out to it, which is now given to the world. A sale (by the Deputy Commissioner of Tezbrusaugar) of the effects of the deceased Pekoe Tips, placed me in possession of a number of diaries, notes and other manuscripts. As I became possessed of "lot No. 13, perishable property" consisting of a flannel cricketing suit, eaten by white ants; two shirts; a broken revolver; one plated spur; and a tin box full of old papers, for the sum of five rupees nine annas and six pie; and as I have selected and sent home to his sorrowing relatives the only private documents I could find in the tin box full of old papers, I consider myself fully justified in publishing such scraps amongst the remaining papers as are suitable for publication. It is a pity they are crude and fragmentary; the lamented death of their writer before he could put his notes and memoranda into shape, makes many allusions to people and events of current interest at date of the diaries or notes, now unmeaning. I have not had the time to make, as might be made, a connected and interesting story out of these notes and diaries, full of interesting information about the old days of tea. His papers not being dated or methodically arranged, it would have been difficult to separate his first impressions from his matured opinions. He had been many years in tea, it is evident; and made voluminous notes. But he wanted method and system, poor corpse, as so many planters do: I have had to take his notes pretty much just as they came to hand.

With this apology for the form of the following chapters, I withdraw, to allow Mr. Pekoe Tips to speak for himself.

II.—VOYAGE UP.

I LEFT Calcutta in the steamer *Pioneer*, bound for Tezbrusaugar. We went down the same river, the Hooghly, which I had recently come up in the *Blenheim*, for some distance, and then turned off into a lot of winding, tortuous, narrow rivers, sometimes widening out into great estuaries, and sometimes so narrow that we could hardly pass. These creeks and rivers are called the Sanderbands.

The *Pioneer* is a curious sort of vessel. The "poop" is forward in this wrong-ended boat; the saloon is on the upper deck, on top of the cabins, with canvas curtains called *purdahs* to close in the sides, and with a tarpaulin awning on a bamboo framework overhead as a roof. The saloon table is built in over a long opening in the deck which forms a sort of skylight over the passage between the cabins below. When you sit down to meals, your legs are over this open skylight; and I don't think it is a very nice arrangement for ladies. The cabins, opening out from this passage on each side, are separated from each other by venetian partitions, not by solid bulkheads. This is for coolness I suppose, but it is not ver private. People in India don't seem to think much of privacy. In Calcutta they never seem to shut the doors of their bedrooms, but have only one of those curtains called *purdah* hanging in the doorway; and native servants appear to walk in and out whenever they like.

Forward of the saloon and of the cabins are clear spaces, both on the upper and lower decks, some thirty or forty feet long. The lower space is occupied by the fore-hatch, the capstan, which does duty as a windlass for weighing anchor, and the cable range. The upper deck is a sort of promenade and lounging place for the passengers; on it is the wheel, connected by long chains with the rudder away aft (there is no tiller); and from here the pilots and the captain steer the ship. We have two huge barges, lashed one on each side, in tow. They call them flats, and their commanders "flat-captains"; but they don't seem to mind it. On these flats most of the cargo is carried. * * * * *

Through the dreary dismal Sanderbands at last, and arrived at a place called Kushtia, where we took on board some more passengers. These had arrived from Calcutta by rail in one night, while we had been a week coming round. I was so tired of the winding narrow creeks, the mud banks, the dense jungle, and the general loneliness, that I was delighted to get into more open water, and have more companions.

The captain and his wife had been my only associates so far. There were others on board to talk to; the engineers, and the "flat-captains"; but when the steamer-captain's wife saw me talking to any of these, she would call me away, and told me I ought not to associate with them. I cannot quite understand this: the steamer captains must have been in command of a flat before they were promoted. Auntie, who had been many years in India,—indeed it was through some Indian friends of hers I got my situation on a tea garden,—used to tell me about "caste"; but I always thought that caste only divided the natives into classes. I begin to see that there is a good deal of "caste" prejudice amongst Europeans also.

Five passengers got on board at Kushtia, an officer of some regiment in Assam, and his wife, a doctor, and two others; one of whom, to my delight, turned out to be stanley, who had come out in the *Blenheim* with me. He was going up to another garden, higher up in Tezbru-saugar, but had been delayed in Calcutta. I am so glad he had managed to catch me up again; we shall have a lot of fun going up together. The other passenger is Johnson, a planter, a few years older than Stanley or I. He has been out in tea some years, talks the language, and knows all about tea making. He says it is awfully easy. You have only just got to tell the *Mohurrir* to *jaldi chalau;* see that the tea *teklas máro* the *páth* all right; give the tea-house *sirdar* a licking if the tea gets burnt on the *dhols;* and you are sure to get on well. It sounds very easy, but all these strange words puzzle Stanley and me a good deal. The only nuisance is the beastly climate, Johnson says. He has been very ill with "jungle fever," as he calls it; and has been away for a sea trip to get better. He carries a handful of quinine loose in a paper in his pocket, and often takes a good large pinch of it, whenever he feels "queer." He sometimes takes this quinine dry, from the palm of his hand, but generally mixes it in a pint of beer. He looks very yellow and thin still, though he says he is all right now. I hope I shall not get jungle fever; although Johnson says I will soon lose my rosy cheeks about which he chaffs me a good deal. His own get pretty red towards evening, after several doses of quinine in beer, and a good deal of brandy. He gets through a good deal of this latter, and says everyone has to do so, to keep out malaria. I am sure I shall get very drunk, if I have to keep out malaria the way he does; but he says I will soon get used to it.

Stanley and I had rather a lark last night at Gauhati, and I got into a fine row over it this morning. Captain Jones and his wife have the next cabin to ours; I got Stanley into mine for company. Jones went ashore last night after dinner to see some friends, brother officers he said. He stayed very late; at least he had evidently promised his wife to be on board again sooner than he did come; for she was anxiously looking out for him. At last she retired to her cabin; Stanley and I turned in too. After a while I heard her voice "Mr. Tips! Mr. Tips!" "What can I do for you?" I said, as I opened my cabin door and popped my head out. She had done the same thing;—so we both popped our heads in again very rapidly, neither of us being very heavily attired. "Do *please* go and see if my husband has come on board," she continued, through the venetian cabin partitions. We heard some talking and laughing on the lower deck abaft the cabins so Stanley and I went out to see who it was. There was Jones, sure enough, with Johnson and a couple of men from the shore, having "just another little one" before they separated for the night, although they had hardly room for it I should have thought: they all seemed pretty full. We stayed there listening to their chaff and talk, and forgot poor Mrs. Jones's anxiety till presently we heard a "still small voice," with a gradually *crescendo* effect,—"Harry! *Harry!!* HARRY!!! are you *ever* coming to bed to-night?"

That dispersed our little gathering like a shell. "Guess you're wanted, Harry" said the shore people; and with a cheery good night, away they went. They were out of the line of fire; but "Harry" didn't look half so cheerful as he walked forward to his cabin, trying to look as if he had only been drinking soda water all evening. Didn't he get it just! and we heard every word. We coughed and made as much noise as we could; I called out once "Give him half a chance;" but Mrs. J. was so irate she took no heed of us. Gradually the storm subsided into sulks on one side and repentance and contrite affection on the other. "Do forgive me, Nellie! Give me a kiss, darling, *do*." No reply. "Only one! just a little one! just to show you're not angry with me." "But I *am* angry with you, Sir!" most emphatically. "Nellie, pet! only *one* kiss;" and so on *ad infinitum*. This was worse than the scolding; we couldn't stand this sort of thing. At last in reply to a fervent "Only one, Nellie! I can't go to sleep without it," Stanley shouted "Give him one for Heaven's sake, Nellie! None of us can go to sleep without it!" There was silence after that. Jones said no more anyhow; but I'm almost sure I heard a distinct titter from "Nellie."

Jones was awfully mad to-day and came to me boiling over with rage, saying I had insulted his wife, and that he had a great mind to box my ears well; I was a most impertinent boy, &c., &c. He must have known it was Stanley's voice, not mine; but Stanley is much bigger than I am; a fine handsome fellow too; so Jones thought it was safer to bully me. His wife knew well enough who it was, for she blushed, and laughed, and called Stanley an "awfully wicked boy" when she met him this morning.

* * * * * *

[There are several pages of description of the journey up by steamer; notes on the natives, the jungles on the bank, the sandbanks and the alligators, the first sight of the snows and the different places passed. But the Assam route is now so well known that I spare the reader Mr. Pekoe Tips' crude observations. The next paper is evidently a draft of a letter to his friend Stanley, who had gone on higher up the river, and describes his landing and arrival on his garden. Stanley's reply, giving *his* first impressions of tea and tea life, which is attached to this draft, had evidently been kept as a contrast.]

III.—THE LANDING.

YOU must remember old boy, what we thought —and said—of Assam, when the *Pioneer* anchored off that mudbank, and the Captain called out 'Tips my boy! here's your destination.' I thought, as you did, that he was up to some of his usual games, and was tryin g to give me a 'sell' again, as he had done once or twice before. But it was no joke this time! Well, to cut it short; you know how I was landed, with the enormous jungle growing right down to the edge of the perpendicular bank above the water! hardly room to stand, much less to walk round in. Not a habitation in sight on land; on the river, nothing but that wretched little 'iron boat' as the skipper called it, with its crew of half a dozen more or less naked black fellows.

When the steamer disappeared round the bend of the river, and I was left, a sort of revised edition of Robinson Crusoe, with an utterly incapable 'man Friday' in the shape of that ass of a *Khansamah* the agents engaged for me in Calcutta, I felt awfully down. I could not talk to the men in the iron boat. The *Khansamah*, in his usual assinine way, attempted to explain my English, which he did not understand, to the men in his own language which they did not understand. I had my boxes and roll of bedding piled up on the only few feet of available space clear of jungle, near. Visions of snakes, tigers, elephants, *et hoc genus omne*, filled my mind. I don't mind letting on to you, old fellow, as you're not likely to meet any of the old boys up your way and get up a chaff against me, that I just sat down on a portmanteau on the bank there, and felt—well, awfully 'snivelly,' you know!

After a while I roused up a bit, wondering what I should do, and how I was ever to get up to my garden. The Calcutta agents had not prepared me for anything of this kind. They said arrangements would be made to meet me at my destination. Pretty arrangements! No one in the country seemed to know of, or care for, my existence. Luckily the Captain's wife had given me some preserved provisions and biscuits in tins, so I was not afraid of starving. I thought this was very kind of her, giving me these things, but I had to pay for them all afterwards.

I went down on board the 'iron-boat' and, with some trouble, got the men to help me to carry my things on board of her. I did not like my surroundings much on the bare deck of a little boat, with nothing overhead but a tarpaulin awning, and right amongst all the black fellows, who didn't smell over pleasant, and who smoked, oh! such *stinking* tobacco! But it was better than lying out on the bank all night, which was the only other chance I had. It is no use dwelling on the miseries of the night I spent. I have been told since that I was 'denced well off;' and I suppose all this is part of the luxuries of the gorgeous East, and the pleasure of a planter's life which we used to hear about at home. I had some tinned salmon, mixed with a mess of greasy *dhal* and rice which my servant got for me from the boatmen, for dinner; and fixing up a mosquito curtain the best way I could under the tarpaulin, I turned in. But the mosquitoes got at me somehow; they always do;

the boatmen smoked, smelt, grunted, and made abnormal noises all night;—and altogether I never was so miserable in my life before.

About noon next day, after some more salmon and greased rice, and several hours of dismal 'mopes,' a curious sort of craft came round the corner, and the men on it brought me a letter from Mr. Ribiera, my manager, saying he had sent this boat down to take me up to the factory. The boat was made of two canoes lashed alongside of each other with a bamboo platform over both, and a curved mat roof over that again. It was called a *mar*. Delighted at some prospect of regaining civilisation, I hurried my things on to this novel arrangement and tried to make a start at once. But I had to wait till the men had cooked their food, so had plenty of time to make myself comfortable, arranging my boxes and bedding so as to make a sort of little cabin for myself.

I need not enlarge upon the weariness of the journey up the river to the factory. It took two days, besides the afternoon of the day we started; the men poling the craft along with bamboos—walking along a sort of narrow ledge—the edge of the bamboo platform outside the mat roof, to do so. I had varieties of tinned things to eat, mixed with the rice the boatmen gave me, and the biscuits. That patent various-bladed knife of mine you used to chaff me about came in very handy in cutting the throats of Bologna Sausage tins and other similar wild animals. I opened a box which had some school-books in, and absolutely read up a lot of botany—freshening my mind for tea gardening, you know; and when I was tired of that I had a shy at some Euclid and Algebra. You may pretty well guess I hadn t any novels in that box,—or any other,—or I would not have been so studious. Its astonishing what a lot of dry reading a fellow can wade through, when he has absolutely nothing else to do; nothing between him and total vacuity of mind.

In the intervals of my curious meals and still more curious studies, I pictured to myself the pleasures of arriving at my destination. I had been told I would have to rough it a little, but I rather liked that part of the idea. Hadn't I read all about this sort of life in the Boys' Own Magazine, Kingston's and Ballantine's stories for boys, and Mayne Reid's novels! I knew exactly what was in store for me; and rejoiced at the prospect. A charming cottage with verandahs all trellis-work and creepers, and a lovely flower garden in front; one or two jovial young fellows of my own age to chum with; a manager whom I would at first look up to with reverential awe, but presently, as I grew older and more experienced, would get quite pleasant with: a crowd of black fellows,—*kulis*, *chuprassis*, *peons*, *jemadars*, *sirdars* and *teklas*—I did not know who and what they all were, but I knew I was to order them all about, and be their ruler and guide. I quite longed to be at my post, and feel that I was doing my duty, and earning my pay.

I feel as if a little of the ardour had been taken off my sentiments and ambitions now; but I must let you judge for yourself. On the third day the boat arrived at what I was told was the *ghât*.

There were no *pakka* steps such as my short stay in Calcutta had associated with my idea of a *ghât*. There was nothing but a break in the same everlasting jungle I had passed for the last three days; and a mud track up through that break. I landed, over my boot-tops in mud; ploughed up the bank; and saw a devious track about a foot wide through the tall grass in front of me. The men commenced tumbling my things out of the boat on to the mud, and signed to me to go on to the bungalow. I understood what "bungalow" meant, so went on hopefully along the winding path through the jungles followed by my servant and one of the boatmen. Presently we emerged on an open space; the track became a sort of undecided and very muddy attempt at a road; a few huts were seen, right and left, which the boatman with me explaned were "coolie-lines;" the huts of the coolies I presumed. Further on, we came to a couple of longer and larger grass huts, more pretentious looking, and with a clear, mud-plastered, space between them. *Sá gark*," said my boatman; my servant interpreted this, "—house for tea make." A few yards further, and we come to a rough and very crooked bamboo fence, with a few plantain trees growing inside it. A path struck off through the fence, at right angles to the road we followed, leading to a large low-eaved grass hut, with an open space, and a gong on a bamboo trinngle, before it. "*Bungalow, Sahib*," said my guide; and the bungalow it was! Oh! sacred shade of my sainted aunt! Where were my poetic visions now? The charming cottage was a wretched looking grass hut; the trellised verandah was a pile of unevenly raised mud, with six crooked posts supporting the low eaves in front, and the bare reed walls of the hut at the back; the lovely garden was a sea of mud with a bamboo scaffolding supporting a brass gong as its only flower. The jovial companions! Where were they? The revered and austere manager? But stop, old boy! this scene should be dramatised, to give it full effect. I wish I could do it.

Picture to yourself your humble servant, with a mixture of disappointment at the surroundings, hope for the future, and a becoming respect for his manager all in his heart,—and his hat in his hand,—stepping up the mud pile which formed the floor of his future residence; passing through the verandah into the central hall; and gazing round, timidly enquiring, at the decidedly dirty and poverty-stricken looking furniture of the room. No one visible: "guggle-guggle-guggle" from the one side-room, suggestive of the boatmen's smoking.

"Who's there?" says a voice from within. Tips, doubtingly, and but half re-assured, replies, "Its me, sir; the new assistant, Mr. Tips. Can I come in? Are you Mr. Ribiera?"

"Oh yes! come along in. D—n glad to see you, come on: don't mind me. Shake hands, young fellow: I'll make you comfortable, never fear; sit here and have a pull."

And this is what I saw, Stanley. I lifted a rough brown blanket which hung in front of the hole in the reed wall which served as a doorway; and there was Mr. Ribiera. A big stout man, almost as dark as the coolies that brought me up in the boat, dressed in thin muslin night clothes—*paijama* and *kurta* I now know they are called—with his dark, fat legs and arms showing through them; sitting on the edge of a bed,—*such* a dirty bed too;—

with a woman, a little darker than himself, but in much cleaner and whiter clothes, and with a lot of silver ornaments about her, sitting beside him. They were having alternate pulls out of a *hukah*; and it was to *this* his hospitable invitation extended! "Sit here and have a pull!"

Stanley, old man, I felt sick. *This* was the manager I was to revere and look up to! I made one manful try to face circumstances. I shook hands with him. I bowed to the—the—*creature* on the bed; and said, "Mrs. Ribiera, I presume. The agents didn't mention I should have the pleasure of living with a married man, and of ladies' society." You, see old fellow, I did my best to face the thing. I didn't know as much of Tezbrusaugar ways as I do now! Ribiera shook his fat sides laughing. "Ha! ha! ha! Mrs. Ribiera! so the agents didn't tell you I was married?"

* * *

IV.—THE REVERSE OF THE PICTURE.

YOU dear Misused old Tips,—How do I pity you! You seem to have had decidedly a bad time of it, one way and another. I certainly pitied you, left stranded on the sands of Sunkeri Mukh, with nothing but jungle and the "iron" boat and its crew to console you. I have often wondered during the last few weeks, how you got on to your destination. Your letter received the other day has enlightened me as to your progress in Assam civilization, so far. By the way, before I go any further, how is Mrs. Ribiera? does she improve on aquaintance?

Your experiences of Tezbrusaugar are, I hope, somewhat unique. Anyhow, very few men, to judge by my experience—only as old as your own—meet with the reception you did. My advent on my garden was under distinctly different auspices. When we left you, and lamented your sad fate, at Sunkeri Mukh, we steamed on two days more before I met *my* fate. I landed, something like yourself, on what Paddy would call a "dissolute island." There was no connection with the main land: no comfortable bungalow, shed, or even hut in sight; nothing but jungle. Not even an iron boat, as in your case. But there our parallel ends, I think. Even on the "dissolute island" I found, when I in my turn was shunted ashore by the benevolent Captain, a letter, half a dozen coolies, and a pony, awaiting me. The letter informed me that the coolies would carry my luggage, or as much of it as I urgently needed, on to the garden where my boss resided. The pony would do ditto, for my own *corpus vile*. The "dissolute island" was easily negotiated. About half a mile of sand and reedy grass intervened between where the steamer landed me and a *suti*, or side stream, of our noble river. There was one of those double barrelled canoes you rightly call a *már*, to get across the *suti* in. Once crossed, pony, coolies, and all in the one venture, I cantered on for some miles on what would be called a fairly decent sort of village lane at home (raised up and with the hedges knocked off) until I came to my destination.

Now then, old Tips, how does *my* bungalow and its surroundings, and *my* manager and his belongings, fit yours? For about half a mile I had been cantering along the road, through tea on each side, before reaching the bungalow; which, as it was on a slight hill or elevation, had been visible for some time.

In front of the house was a very neatly kept garden, laid out in beds of regular shape, with little paths round them. The verandah is partly trellised, between the posts, and some pretty creepers are growing over the bamboo-work. Brick steps, plastered over, lead up to this verandah, or rather porch, I should call it, as it projects out some 20 feet from the ordinary verandah running along the front of the house; and is practically an extra room, with split bamboo curtains, called *chiks*, to let down and close it in, or roll up and open it out at will. The house itself is the ordinary shape—an oblong, divided laterally right through. This seems to be the standard Assam plan. There is a bedroom at each end with a bathroom behind each; and the two centre rooms represent a dining and sitting room.

Neat but somewhat faded damask purdahs hang at all the doors. The windows are unglazed, but closed with a mesh of fine bamboo work and have clean white muslin curtains to them.

The verandah and porch are matted with a coarser kind of interweaving of the ever useful bamboo, as are the two bedrooms. But the centre rooms have cotton carpets and gaily coloured rugs over the matting; and in the bedrooms there are a couple of these rugs also. Good solid furniture in all the rooms,—nothing superfluous but everything necessary: quite a handsome dressing table in the boss' room, I noticed. In the sitting-room, a couple of couches and some cane chairs covered with chintz; a couple of tables with albums and nick-nacks on them, a large and well filled bookcase, and positively a harmonium. How is that for high, in the wilderness, Tips my boy! But enough of describing the place; it is a very comfortable, plainly but neatly furnished bungalow. I only wish I had to stay there, instead of being shunted to this out-garden, where the bungalow isn't much better than the one you describe; only I flatter myself it is neater and cleaner.

As I rode up to the porch I saw a couple of men, dressed in white trousers, and flannel shirts very open at the neck, with the trousers tucked inside the socks over the boots (this seems to be the correct planter's dress) reclining on two long cane chairs. These proved to be the manager of the head garden or factory, and the superintendent of the company; and they speedily made me thoroughly comfortable and at home.

"Very glad to see you, Stanley," said the shorter man of the two, getting up from his long chair and shaking my hand heartily. "I'm Edwards, and this is Reed," he continued, introducing the taller man with a wave of his hand,—"the manager here, you know. How did the pony bring you along? What will you have to drink?" After getting outside a bottle of Bass, and blowing a genial cloud together, during which they asked me a lot of questions about Calcutta and the trip up the river, while I asked them a lot about life on the garden,—we seemed to have known each other for years. My things came up in a couple of hours; I had a comfortable tub in Edwards' room; relegated my collar and necktie to the shadowy realms of the past, by his advice, and came out in the regulation planter's rig, just in time for a sherry and bitters before dinner.

The dinner was not a very swell one, the staple consisting of what Edwards called the "everlasting *murghi*." For vegetables we had a sort of pumpkin called *rungalow*. Potatoes are only to be got from the steamers, now and then, as a treat. Bread there was none, of course; as a substitute there was a sort of nondescript cake made of rice flour, and plenty of cabin biscuits. They tell me that the food supply is the great drawback to life in Tezbrusaugar. The only things obtainable locally are fowls, ducks, and rice; these are plentiful and cheap; but everything else must be got up from Calcutta by steamer. And as the steamer visits are, like angels, few and far between, it occasionally happens that fellows get clean eaten and drunk out, and are reduced to a monotonous diet of fowls and rice washed down by river water only, for a while, till next steamer comes up.

It will take me sometime I fancy to learn to look on inned provisions as luxuries. At present I prefer the fowls and ducks; but, as Edwards said, I shall no doubt get precious tired of them when I have eaten so many hundreds of them that I feel an inclination to go crowing and quacking all over the place.

After dinner we had a long talk about things in general. They rather laugh at the gardens down your way, Tips, my boy, and say that unless you are a pretty spry young man you are likely to came to grief. The smart old gentleman—we wont mention his name—who promised your confiding aunt such a grand situation for you in a splendid tea company, is not quite so disinterestedly benevolent as he appears, if all Edwards says is correct. Didn't the poor old lady buy some Central Tezbrusaugar shares,—at a premium too? I think you told me something about it. As far as I can gather from what they say here, that pious old impostor has got quite a knack of inducing the fatherless and the widow to purchase shares in the companies he floats; so maiden aunts would be good fish for his net too. Giving "our dear nephew" a splendid opening (how you appreciate the splendour of the opening your first letter shows) was a capital bait. They say the old ruffian has made a princely fortune by buying up gardens here and there that had never managed to make a profit,—getting them dirt cheap of course. This was the first step. Then a few hundred acres near each old garden was cleared, or supposed to be cleared, and planted, or said to be so. Next, a grand prospectus was issued; some of the particular Calcutta initiates floated the company; the promoter *vel* proprietor took so much cash and so much in shares; and all was serene. A good dividend was declared, first year: no one would know it was paid out of the capital. Shares were at a premium; and the orignal seller of the property and the ring who floated the company got out of the boat very quietly but promptly; generously letting their friends (including the fatherless and the widow aforesaid) have a chance at this real good thing. And so all was still lovely and beautiful, for them. The end is not yet. I guess you'll be in the last act of the play yourself, from all I hear.

Good bye, Tips! Take care of yourself; don't run away with Mrs. Ribiera; and let me know how you get on.

Yours ever,
G. Stanley.

V.—TIPS' DIARY.

I HAVE been here over a month now, and am supposed to be able to have formed an idea of how I like the place and the work. I like it so much that I haven't had the heart to open my diary since I came here, till tonight. I don't think I was fastidious at home ; we don't belong to the "first families," nor are we county people; so I cannot be accused of aristocratic proclivities and tastes. But I must confess to a weakness for cleanliness and common decency. I have a lingering memory of table cloths and their use. Table napkins I have sternly repudiated, since the first night I dined here. Oh! that dinner ; shall I ever forget it? A table that had once been varnished,—teak wood I should think as far as I could judge through the encrusted dirt of ages that coated it,—three or four odd plates (two of them soup-plates) of the violent blue, yellow, and red pattern sometimes seen in kitchens, a yellow greasy mass —or mess—of curry in a slop bowl, and a gritty heap of half-husked rice in a dish ; sundry very brassy spoons and forks and, floating around and penetrating through all other flavours, the (to me) disgusting odour of the *huka* which the *mem-sahib* (who sat at table with us) had indulged in a few final whiffs of just before dinner, to give her an appetite. The plate placed in front of me had apparently not been washed since it was made. The memories of a decade of past breakfasts and dinners hung solidly to its sides. In a weak moment I ventured to remark,—"Mr. Ribiera, would you mind asking your servant just to wipe this plate a little." He laughed,—a great, oily, jovial laugh: I must admit he is a genial sort, according to his lights. "Ar-reh! man," said he, "you're very particular. You soon get used to this kind *khannah* when you stop longer in Tezbrusaugar." Then he turned to his *khansamah*—a Bengali coolie apparently—promoted from the lines I have since heard, on account of a family connection; and said something. Whereupon the man took my plate; looked at it sideways in the light of the oil-lamp to find out what I objected to; and finally, picking up a corner of his nether garment—*dhoti* I have heard it called—gave the plate a dry rub with that fearful weapon, and clumped it down before me again with a grunt, as much as to say "I hope you are satisfied now."

That is why I don't ask for table napkins. I prefer to use my own pocket handkerchiefs.

I have got used to these little trifles now: I am surprised now, when I come to think, how many of the bad habits of civilisation—and cleanliness—I have learnt to get rid of. I sleep very comfortably in the corner of our "dining-room" on half a dozen tea boxes; my mosquito curtain tied up to bamboos stuck in holes in the floor; with the balmy odours of a week's curries and *hukas* hanging like a pall over and round me.

I have educated Ribiera into using one of my clean bed sheets for a table cloth; it hides the dirt on the table and I've got my own little stock of crockery and cutlery in use; while my Calcutta servant certainly improved the *cuisine* a trifle, and kept things cleaner for a time. But he is gone, alas! I was afraid he would not stand it long and I am left to the mercies of a boy who knows nothing and who can talk no language but his own. I have learned a few words of the language, but it is uphill work. The worst of it is Ribiera expects me to do such a lot, and I can't get on without being able to talk. "Now I got assistant" says old Fatty. "I'm going to be *burra sahib.* You got to learn your work, Tips; and best way to learn is to go find out for yourself." And so the old sinner shunts me out into the garden, and into the tea-house; and I'm sure all the men—and the women too, which is worse—laugh at me. I don't know anything about it yet. All Ribiera does of out-door work is to look after the thatch-cutting. I'm sure I don't know why it wants the *burra sahib* to look after a lot of women out in the jungle cutting bundles of thatching grass. I should have thought he would do better looking after the hoeing or pruning, which he leaves to me. Even the tea-house work, I am sure, wants better than my care. The tea I am getting out of the bins is quite musty, and I don't think they fire it half enough before packing. It can't be good when it gets home. But Ribiera just says "What d'you know, man? Everything sells rupee a pound, so what's the good of bothering. You let the tea *sirdar* alone." Then again, here is March, pruning nearly all done, and in another month they say the "flushes" will be on, *i.e.*, the new tea leaves on the bushes; and there is an *awful* lot of last year's tea in the bins yet. I wonder they can't pack it as they make it.

Ribiera has gone off to Rikitijan, "an out-garden" of this division, for two or three days; so I have the place to myself and am picking up heart to make some notes of my surroundings and my progress as a planter. But oh! what a different life to what I anticipated. Stanley's lines seem to have fallen in much pleasanter places. When I got Harriet's letter the other day, asking me how I enjoyed my new life in the wild frontiers of India: how many *rajahs* and *nabobs* I knew; how many elephants and horses I had; what pretty things was I going to send her home; and how long I would be in making my fortune and coming home a *nabob* myself; I just laughed at myself and my then grand ideas. But it was a very sore laugh, on the wrong side of my mouth.

I had to write her a whole lot of nonsense in reply, and break things very gently. I told her I would be at least *ten* years making money enough to go home with, instead of the five she hopes for. I wonder if she will wait ten years for me? Heigho! She will be eight and twenty then. I dared not tell how very different things really are to what we used to imagine in our *chateaux en Tezbrusaugar*, when we talked of my coming out.

I think it is to relieve my feelings of the strain the white lies I told her have left on them, that I feel like scribbling all my real impressions in my diary tonight.

I am all alone. The *kerani mohurrir* (English writer) has gone sometime ago. He is a very good little fellow; talks and writes a little English, but not well. We have made a bargain: whenever I am alone, he is to come up and give me an hour; I teach him English, and he teaches me Assamese. I am trying to learn to write it, as Barnstable, who is the Superintendent of the Partigarh concern near here, and a first-rate man I think, says every planter ought to read and write the language. To compare with future wrinkles (Barnstable says there will be great changes in tea soon) I will note a day's work here; and another day I will jot down what I have heard about manufacturing which we shall begin in a month or so.

We don't get up very early in the morning here; Ribiera likes to take it easy and so we don't get *chota hazri* till eight o'clock or so. The coolies are all supposed to be out at work by that time, and my first duty, before breakfast, is to go round the work. The road out to the garden from the bungalow is little better than a path through jungle. The grass is growing up now a little, after having been burned off a month or two ago: in the rains the jungle here will be very high. I wonder if it would not pay, both for the look of the thing, and the health of coolies, to keep this jungle cleared. But my friend the *Kerani Mohurrir* says they can't keep the garden clean in the rains, let alone jungle paths. Once out to the garden I walk round the hoeing first to see that it is properly done. I was very helpless at first, but I begin to understand what is wanted now,—a good clean stroke of the hoe, well turned over to bury the grass and expose the roots, and to clean out round the roots of the bushes. And I can explain myself to the coolies a little better than I used to. Then there is still a little pruning going on—Barnstable says we are very late—so I go and have a look at that. There is not much care wanted here apparantly; the big shears, like an exaggerated pair of scissors, soon clip off superfluous twigs and leaves, and leave the bush shorn into a sort of cup-like shape, slightly hollow in the middle, which seems to be the orthodox thing in pruning. Barnstable says the whole system is barbarous, and he is going to prune with knives next year; but Ribiera laughs at this, as at many others, what he calls, new fangled notions.

I now walk back, past the bungalow again, to the tea-house. First, I have to see how many logs the buffaloes have dragged in; and then have a look at the sawyers. We are to make 400 boxes this year: the buffaloes drag in two *rogu* logs every evening; and two pair of sawyers are employed cutting these logs into half inch planks. It is so funny to see them work, the lazy style they tackle to anything.

In the tea-house I have to see how the firing is going on, and weigh as many boxes as are ready filled, to be soldered down. Then back to the bungalow, a bath, and breakfast.

My afternoon is generally divided between the garden and the tea-house in much the same way, with less work in the garden and more tea to weigh in the tea-house. Then the boxes are all nailed down and marks stencilled on them, and the tea-house closed for the evening. The *hazri mohurrir* comes up to the bungalow and drones out an incomprehensible sort of muster roll of work done, or rather number of men employed that day. The *jemadar* gets orders about tomorrow's work the *keranni* pays out any *tikka* pice and gets his rough or petty cash book initialled : and so we turn to dinner with what appetite we may.

VI.—HIS FIRST SPREE.

I GOT back yesterday from Partigarh, Barnstable's garden, after a three days holiday; or what they call "a little spree." Barnstable got up a lot of stores by a *màr* from Sunkeri Mukh; and as appears to be the custom in Tezbrusaugar, he invited a few men over to try his new supplies. I don't think he has much liquor left. This also seems to be a custom in Tezbrusaugar. When a man gets up his supplies, his neighbours gets news of it, and, invited or not, they generally manage to drop in casually, one after another. A good many of them stay, too, as long as they can get anything to drink; and the *mohurrirs* and *jemadars* look after their gardens meanwhile.

Barnstable is said to be one of the "coming men;" a very steady hard-working fellow he certainly is, but we had a pretty lively time of it for three days, nevertheless. When I got there, after a few miles jaunt through two rivers and along a belt of heavy forest on an elephant, I found about a dozen men there before me. A few I had met before, the rest were strangers to me; some of them from a considerable distance. Ribiera gave me a couple of days' leave "to go and see a little life," he said. I may have seen "life" but it certainly is a life I don't care to see too much of. As I arrived they had apparently finished breakfast; and were scattered about the dining-room and verandah in all sorts of attitudes and on all sorts of chairs, smoking, playing cards and drinking. My advent was hailed by a shout from all hands. One big red-bearded man—

Simons was his name—picked me up as I slipped awkwardly off the elephant on its sitting down in front of the bungalow; and after nearly knocking me down, with a hearty slap on the shoulders, cried out: "Here's the young'un come at last, Barnstable! what'll you have to drink?" My mild suggestion, "I should like a cup of tea, thank you," was received with derisive shouts. "By Jove!" cried Simons, "the young'un wants a cup of tea! Poor little dear! you must get out of these weak-minded habits of yours, out here. Tea will never keep fever out Tips my boy, take my word for it; I haven't tasted tea for years," He certainly looked as if he were in the habit of drinking something stronger than tea. All the colour in his face seemed to have centred in his nose.

A foaming glass of beer was shoved into my hand. "Drink it up young'un," said Simons; while a young fellow seated by, chanted in a semi-maudlin way—"Take it Bob take it, its better than tea! I used to like tea, too, Tips" this young man added, "but I've got over that weakness, haven't I Simons?"

"That you have with a vengeance," said Simons. "I'll back you to drink anything intoxicating or poisonous against the oldest hand in the district; you've done pretty well for a yearling."

I drank down my beer, and was glad of it, too; for I had had a tedious ride, not being accustomed to elephant travelling. There is no formality in Tezbrusaugar society evidently. Introductions are unnecessary; men you never saw before, call you by your name at once,—if they even don't christen you with a nickname, and they knock you about with the utmost familiarity, at sight. I think I must have had more than one glass of beer before Barnstable got some breakfast brought back for me; for I found myself talking tremendously "big" about what I used to do in the running and jumping line at school; and was accepting challenges to do all sorts of impossible things pretty freely, when he put his hand on my shoulder and said: "Come along and have something to eat, Tips; and don't let these fellows roast you too much at first; you'll be pretty well done before they've finished you." He came and sat with me, while I ate my breakfast and talked so kindly and sensibly to me, that I felt I liked him better than ever. He gave me a quiet hint not to let the fellows give me too much to drink and said, "Have your fling you must, of course; once in a way a spree hurts no one, especially a youngster. But keep a level head; steady down when its over; and don't get into the habit of drinking for drink's sake, as so many fellows do out here. A little liquor for fun's sake won't hurt you once in a way, if you don't get into the habit of it."

We had a very jolly afternoon, one way and another. Shooting at tea boxes out in the compound with a revolver, cards for some of the fellows, and a little attempt at jumping when the sun got low, passed away the time. There was a good deal of beer mixed with everything; and I am afraid I got more than my share; for when I went to wash for dinner (no one dressed for dinner particularly) I found my head was rather "fuzzy;" soaking it in a big bowl of water was extremely pleasant. I don't think I was very sure of what I was saying all the time; and I would have given a good deal to have gone to bed straight, without any dinner. But that was impossible.

At dinner I had something more; what, I hardly know; but I remember trying very hard to keep the lamp on the table stationary in my eyes and to prevent it from resolving itself into two lamps about a foot apart. I didn't succeed very well; it *would* duplicate itself in a most annoying way. There was some singing after dinner, and I was conscious of someone playing a little harmonium that stood in the corner of the room, and playing it very badly, too. This seemed to rouse me a bit. A voice—it seemed to me to come from far off, but it was only the man next me—said, "I heard you could play, Tips?" My tongue wouldn't work very well somehow, but I managed to get out something like "Coursh I can, berrer'n *at* man anyhow." There was a shout of "Tips to the front! Tip us a waltz old man!" and I was escorted to the chair in front of the instrument and plumped down in it. The keyboard waved about and slid helplessly here and there before my eyes; but vigorously concentrating my duplicate vision for a moment, I managed to catch a chord in three flats before the black notes slipped from under my fingers. Once I caught it I held on to it and instinctively dropped into the "Elfin Waltz." The music seemed to steady me a bit and I got on finely. A vision of men whirling round the room, some in couples, some with chairs as partners, and one man dancing a frantic *pas seul;* a confused notion of congratulations, slaps on the back, someone offering me brandy and water, more music, more whirling round, more brandy—and then—blank darkness.

A voice penetrated the obscurity for a moment, it sounded like Barnstable's; "Poor little beggar! let him alone. Its his first spree, he's tight already;" then oblivion.

Sometime afterwards—it might have been hours or days—I woke; or rather I seemed to struggle into this existence from another world wherein I had been tortured for misdeeds in this one. My head throbbed, my tongue felt like fiery parchment; and a strange weight seemed to tie down my limbs; while light tickling sensations seemed creeping here and there over my body and limbs. Was this nightmare or what? I struggled further into consciousness and found it was all too real. Head and tongue sensations were *very* real, and my limbs were tied down in sober reality too. Some of the festive crowd had slipped away from the dining-room, "to have a lark with the young'un." Finding me in a heavy drink-sodden slumber, they proceeded to disencumber me of my garments; tie my hands and feet down; and procuring a paint pot and brush were busily decorating me with spots and stripes as their sweet fancies suggested. As I realised their fell design, rage thoroughly roused and partly sobered me. Lying still a moment to collect my ideas, I found the lashings were all loose. With a feigned sleepy turn I slipped out of them, then with a frantic kick and plunge, I sent two of my tormenters flying; (Simons got a vigorous heel in his "bread-basket" I am delighted to think) and springing out of bed I made a rush for the dressing table. I was in Barnstable's room where he had kindly located me "to keep me out of mischief" as he said, and I knew there were razors there. Seizing one of these deadly weapons I flourished it high in the air. Pale and convulsed with rage; naked; spotted and striped with paint; I must have presented a picture to make a graven image laugh. But I terrified that half-screwed crew, and when Barnstable and one or two of the steady ones, roused from their talk by the row, came in, they found me flourishing a razor, declaiming grandiloquently against their dastardly conduct and daring them to come on now; while some of my audience laughed, some apologised and tried to soothe me down; and Simons, with a rueful look, rubbing his "godown" as he called it, said "By— the young'un's got pluck in him and can kick out well too." Barnstable turned out the crowd, got me calmed down and into bed again, after giving me a big drink of lime juice and water; and so ended my first day "on the spree."

VII.—THE POSTHUMOUS PAPERS OF PEKOE TIPS, ESQ.

THE DIARY AGAIN.

WE are pretty well into the middle of the season now, and I must say I don't like it half as well as the cold weather. It is always raining; everything is damp, moist and unpleasant; clothes get spotted and musty, boots get covered with mildew; insects of marvellous forms and intensely aggravating and smelling powers, swarm round the light of an evening, and, aided by the ever voracious mosquito, make life almost unbearable in the bungalow. Outside it is worse. The roads are simply beds of slush; the high grass on either side wets you as you go through, even though it is not raining. Leeches crawl up your legs from the roots of the jungle and drop down the back of your neck from the tops of it. The soft soil of the tea garden clogs round the boots, till one can hardy lift one's feet; and over and above all, the damp, steamy, muggy heat produces an atmosphere which reminds one of a back kitchen on a washing day, without the cleanly, half pleasant smell of soap-suds. But the tea-house! Words fail me to paint the horrors of that *inferno*. Herein, to the natural heat and steaminess, is added the blaze of two enormous fire-places, filled with logs, over which the tea leaf is "panned"; and the further torture of rows upon rows of; small holes in the floor—*chulas*, they are called—filled with burning charcoal, on which the tea is dried. The damp exuding from the tea leaf, and the peculiar aroma of the tea in its various stages, make the tea-house a fearful place to spend days—and nights too—in, as I have to, in this hot weather.

A day's work in the tea-house in August is enough to take the starch out of most men. It is a veritable rendering of the primeval curse; in very truth have I to earn my bread by the sweat of my brow now-a-days. Early in the morning, long before any reasonable being would get out of bed, of his own free will, I have to be down in the tea-house to see if the leaf is withered sufficiently to begin rolling. The tea *sirdars* come about the same time as I do; then the *teklas* turn up after a while; and the leaf is weighed out to them—20 seers to each man is our rate—and they set to work. Squatting on a mat on the floor, they take a mass of the leaf and roll it about under their hands and arms till it becomes perfectly flaccid. Then smaller lumps of this leaf,—handfuls one might say—are taken up to the rolling tables and manipulated there by the hand only. The rolling tables are long wooden platforms covered with mats; the process of manipulation, with both hands, one alternately backwards and slightly down as the other pushes forward and upwards, seems to require a little skill. I have tried my hand at it, and am gradually learning to do it so as to put a good "twist" on the leaf, which seems to be the desideratum. After all the leaf is thus rolled, a process seldom finished before noon or one o'clock, and often much later if the leaf is unusually wet, it is stacked up in little closely pressed heaps, covered with cloths—sheeting of some sort—and left to ferment, while all hands go to breakfast. By two o'clock we are at it again. The fires are lit under the big pans; the fermented leaf is thrown into the pans in convenient quantities, and tossed rapidly about in them by a tea *sirdar*, armed with a couple of bits of bamboo, so as to heat it thoroughly and yet not allow it to burn by remaining in contact with the heated iron pans. A good deal of judgment is needed here and skill in tossing the leaf about. When the *sirdar* thinks it is "cooked" enough he throws it out into a *dholla*, or flat circular basket, held at the side of the furnace by an attendant coolie; rapidly brushing out all stray scraps with a sort of bamboo whisk to prevent any burning. The load is tossed steaming hot on to the head of one of the rolling tables, along each side of which stand a row of coolies; and the mass is rapidly divided amongst them and rolled by hand in the same manner as the green leaf was in the morning, but for a shorter time. Passing from hand to hand, each giving it a harder roll than the last, it finds its way into another *dholla* waiting at the bottom of the table, and is carried off to the pans again, to be heated and steamed up once more. After the second panning it passes rapidly down the rolling table, to be received again in a *dholla* at the end of it. This time it is carried off to the *chulas* to be dried. The drying is done over the charcoal fires in the little circular holes or fire-places in the mud floor. Over each of these is a basket-work drum, narrow waisted and broad at top and bottom, called a *dhól*. On top of each of these is a flat *dholla* of somewhat open texture on which a certain amount of tea is placed, thinly spread; and covered over by another *dholla*. Great care has to be taken that the fire is perfectly clear; no smoke from half burnt charcoal, or particles of fallen tea must be allowed. From time to time the *dhól* is carefully removed from the fire—the use of the toes to steady the bottom of the *dhól* in moving it, so that no tea may fall into and spoil the fire, is remarkable here,—and placed over another *dholla* to catch falling particles, the tea is stirred round and respread and the *dhól* cautiously replaced on the fire. And so on *ad infinitum*. The drying process is slow and wearisome. Touch and smell are the only guides to a knowledge of when the tea is thoroughly dried and not burnt. One has equally to avoid the Scylla of *kutcha* tea, and the Charybdis of over-firing or burning. Tea *sirdars* are human and subject to human weaknesses. They get sleepy and careless after a long hot day in a temperature of a hundred and anything you like; and on the tea-house assistant lies the onus of seeing that the firing is as near perfection as may be, before putting the dry tea into the temporary bin, whence it has to be weighed into the permanent one and recorded as manufactured tea next morning. It is more often tomorrow morning than not, before I get to bed, to lie and swelter under a mosquito curtain, worn out, over fatigued and utterly washed out, with the prospect of turning out again at four or five; the hum of the voracious mosquito, and the plaintive howl of the jackal lull me to a four hours' sleep. Truly if I had my choice I would choose a more pleasant life than that of a tea-house assistant.

Ribiera makes it pleasant for me at times too. Sometimes I suppose I am as sleepy as the *sirdars;* the tea is a bit green or a trifle burnt occasionally; and as sure as anything *is* a little out of order, old "Fatty" is sure to select that particular morning to come round the place making nasty remarks, and comparing the pleasant life I have of it—nothing to do but sit down comfortable all day under cover and watch the men—with the way he has knocked about all over the garden, rain or shine, to look after the hoeing and plucking, and see when the next flush will be ready.

He must have pretty sharp eyes if he can see the flush coming out on *some* parts of the garden. I had a stroll round on Sunday last, when there was no leaf in on Saturday, and I couldn't see any bushes at all in a good many places. The grass was right over the tea, and yet he is always grumbling that he can't spare extra men for the tea-house as they are wanted at the hoe to keep the jungle down. I think they *are* wanted at the hoe pretty badly. We have not half enough coolies on the place; at least there are not enough at work. The sick list and "charges general" account for a good many. The way these poor beggars die here has been something awful since the rains set in. They are dirty brutes too; there is no possibility of making them keep themselves, their huts, or even their food, clean. Their favourite relish seems to be fish, caught a fortnight ago, and spread out on the roof, or any convenient place handy, to decompose, till it gets a good high flavour. A walk through the lines is no joke. I am getting quite clever at the regulation medical treatment for coolies now. There are, as a rule, only three prescriptions. First day, the native doctor comes up and reports :—

" *Búdhu bemár áse.*" (Budhu is ill) " *Báru, ek* ounce castor-oil *dibo-lage* " is the reply. Second day, Budhu has diarrhœa, or choleraic symptoms ; second prescription " *Dúta* cholera pill *dé.*" Third day native doctor casually remarks : " *Búdhu moril ; ki korim ?*" (Búdhu is dead, what shall I do ?)

The reply is stereotyped :—

" D—n it ! there's another beggar gone ! "

" *Páni-at pélai-dè ! Emahor bhitorot kiman hoise ?* " (Throw him into the river. How many this month.) This sort of thing is getting monotonous. I don't think Tebrusangar is a very healthy climate somehow.

VIII.—THE EDITOR'S SUMMARY.

SINCE I first undertook to edit the mass of MSS which fell to my lot in "lot No. 13, perishable property" at the sale of the poor deceased's effects by the Deputy Commissioner of Tezbrusaugar, I have gradually become oppressed by the consciousness that the task is somewhat beyond my powers. Poor Tips had, apparently, a certain talent for observing his surroundings, and a great facility, with abundant leisure, for making voluminous notes. I cannot publish them *in extenso*, for various reasons. And yet there is a certain amount of interesting information about the tea industry some thirty years or so ago to be dug out of his diaries and letters. The difficulty is somewhat in the nature of *embarres des richesses:* selection becomes trying, while wholesale publication is, as before noted, impossible. With due regard to the feelings of the long-suffering reader, I have decided to wind up the present series of papers with a general summary.

It may be borne in mind that Tips' first introduction to tea was in the days when it was more of a Calcutta share speculation than the serious business, the recognised industry into which it has now developed. Some thirty odd years ago there were a few—very few—good solid companies working on a firm businesslike basis. Tips' friend, Stanley, was in one of these ; and went on rejoicing, and prospered accordingly. To judge from letters and the diary, Stanley stayed in the same company for some eight or ten years, rising in pay and position as time went on, evidently saving money, and "opening out" for himself, judiciously and economically, in conjunction with one or two kindred spirits in the same district. He apparently went home for a year's leave, while poor Tips was still struggling on; and returned, not to his former position, but to manage the flourishing private garden in which he had a share, and which he had helped to open out. Two or three years of this, contemporary with a couple of "good seasons," and high prices, enabled him to retire finally from an active tea life. We hear of him occasionally as paying an occasional cold weather visit to Tezbrusaugar, to look after his growing interests in tea; and to be looked up to and consulted as "Sir Oracle" by those still struggling though the mire. Stanley was one of the successful men; there were a good many of them, one way and another. But we don't hear so much from them as we do from the unsuccessful ones, naturally. The people who win don't shout half so loud as those who lose, as a rule.

The experiences of Pekoe Tips were evidently very different. The Central Tebrusaugar Company would appear to have been one of the numerous companies floated in the good old days, on the strength of a few acres here and there of actual full grown tea bushes, and an additional area, partly imaginary, and partly hastily cleared land done on contract by local labour, with a certain quantity of seed allowed per acre nominally cleared; which seed might, or might not have been planted; and a large percentage of which certainly never came up. A good many of such companies were floated in the good old times. A few astute "old stagers" in Tezbrusaugar, aided by a little ring of brokers and others in the metropolis, managed to make a pretty good thing out of these companies, although the bulk of the shareholders probably objurgate the names and memories of those defunct concerns even unto this day.

The process was remarkably simple ; indeed absolutely touching in its simplicity.

A flourishing prospectus ; so many hundred acres under cultivation ; a few well known names on the board of direction : (some of the names become better known than trusted eventually) ; and the shares were soon taken up. Managers and assistants, all sorts and conditions of men, alike only in their enthusiasm for tea, their profound belief in rapidly making their fortunes out of it, and their equally profound ignorance of everything connected with practically growing or manufacturing it, were readily forthcoming in shoals. Small capitalists rushed to take up the few shares they could command, certain of having discovered a veritable *El Dorado.* Shares were soon at a premium : a dividend the first year or two kept them still on the rise. People were not so particular then as now ; accounts were a nuisance ; auditors a bore : no one except a few interested parties knew or cared where the dividend came from ; if the profit didn't come naturally, there was generally an available balance of capital in hand. As a matter of fact tea in those days did pay handsomely, when there was any genuine backbone in the gardens. Production was small ; prices good ; and purchasers were not so knowing to discern good from evil as they have now become. Professional experts or tea-tasters were unknown; reports on samples, with nasty remaks about liquor, out-turn, fermentation, or flavour, were unheard of. Indian tea was—well, it was Indian tea; and although it was utterly unknown to the actual consumer, it was worth an average rupee a pound to the producer.

I find a curious note in Tips' Diary, a year or two later than the date of my last extract, touching on the profits which his garden was making, at the time his Company was rapidly going to the dogs.

The worst of Tips' papers are that one has to guess at his chronology a good deal; but the following is evidently written shortly before his first collapse and the Company's. Ribiera had left; and Tips, after a year or two's wandering about from one garden to another in the Company, had been appointed as manager at Sunkeri, where he first joined as assistant under Ribiera. He was evidently proud of his charge, and did his best in it. I will let him speak for himself once more.

"Stanley writes and tells me he hears we are likely to smash up. It may be true; but if it is so, all I can say is I don't understand it. It seems to me that my garden, Sunkeri, is making a large profit." (Tips was naturally very proud of his first charge.) "I have got over 150 acres of pretty good tea here now—all clear of jungle too. I've built new lines upon the rising ground near the garden, and away from the low swampy ground near the river, where they were before. I have got the tea-house in better order; new *chulas*, new wooden framed and planked binns lined with zinc sheets, to keep the tea in, instead of the old mat things in which it used to get so musty. And I've done all this out of the same monthly remittance as Ribiera used to get: in fact Rs. 200 a month less, as my pay is that much less than his was. I would like to see what old 'Fatty' would think of the garden and the place now. I don't think he would be very comfortable in the bungalow; he would find it too neat and clean to suit his tastes. What an awful job I had to clean it up!

"As far as I can make out, mygarden here ought to be paying *one hundred per cent.* on the actual local working expenses. My monthly remittance is Rs. 2,000 or Rs. 24,000 for the year. Last year the garden, under Ribiera, made over 3½ maunds per acre; and I shall make 4 maunds this year, if not more. So I am certain of 600 maunds of tea. This at our usual average of a rupee a pound. will bring in Rs. 48,000; just double the expenditure.

"Of course I know that off this has to come freight, paid in Calcutta; and the cost of tea lead and other stores which are currently used up. As for tools and other lasting things, we have had nothing new since I came out, except a few of Barnstable's new-fangled pruning knives. There were 50 new coolies last year; none this. Altogether I think if quarter the profit, 25 per cent. or Rs. 6,000, is allowed for stores and freight, it is more than enough. What on earth becomes of the other 75 per cent., Rs. 18,000, that I am making for the Company on this garden alone? That is what I want to know?"

Poor Tips! that is what a good many other people besides himself wanted to know; but somehow they never found out

EXTRACTS FROM THE CHRONICLES OF TEZBRUSAUGAR.

I.—THE MODEL PLANTER.

THE following papers may be looked on as the combined results of the ancient diaries of poor Pekoe Tips, and of personal reminiscences. For the satisfaction of the timorous, I beg to preface my little stories with the statement that they are *stories*, pure and simple. Should it be necessary to depict a villain let not A or B shriek and rave, saying "That's meant for me!" and thirst for my blood: nor, If I paint a picturesque character—a Bayard, *sans peur et sans reproche*—need moral C and D strut about, laying the flattering unction to their souls that they are therein held up for public admiration. After all the inhabitants of Tezbrusaugar are very like other men. There is a good deal of human nature about them. But there seems to be something in the depressing climate of Tezbrusaugar that softens the epidermis. Some skins become so tender up there that the gentlest fanning of the breath of publicity irritates. Fortunately others remain tough, impervious to keen shafts of ridicule even when avowedly aimed at them; and those within them can absolutely enjoy a joke, even at their own expense, occasionally. But beware of the thin-skinned variety of the *genus homo*: stand not between the wind and their nobility: revile not the elect. These are they whose shrieks are *vox populi;* to obtain their approval, no other attitude than that of respectful admiration is possible. *Experto crede.* The moral whereof is as old as Æsop; coeval with crows, cheese, and foxes. Scribes treating of this variety of mankind must ignore the existence of spots on the sun; to their vision, crows' plumage must be all gloriously radiant, and the corvine voice rival that of the nightingale. Otherwise *garde à vous!* heedless scribe; thou shalt be cut off from among the people, and numbered amongst the transgressors.

Up till very recently I had been under the impression that the planter was like unto other men; subject to like passions and infirmities, as well as endowed with the nobler qualities of human nature. But that is just where I made the mistake. *Humanum est errare* excepts planters, according to my thin-skinned censors. Ordinary men may sin. Planters are perfect. Soldiers and sailors, princes and *padres* may occasionally "look upon the wine when it is red,"—but planters are all blue-ribbon men. A "big drink," and a consequently noisy and somewhat rowdy night, has been known to occur amongst "officers and gentlemen," in a mess-room. But a Tezbrusaugar bungalow is dedicated to piety and peace; and the sound of midnight revelry is never heard therein. Frail man in general may lapse from virtue: but the planter is a very Joseph, fleeing from every temptation.

Our friends with the thin-skin may occasionally read a novel, (if such a proceeding be compatible with their high moral rectitude) wherein there is a villain; or in which Bacchanalian scenes are depicted; or the plot whereof hinges on a seduction, or a *liaison* of a doubtful character. They never protest that the class treated of in that novel are being maligned;

they solemnly sigh over the wickedness of human nature as the plot thickens; they reach for the third volume, and thank heaven they are not as other men are. But when the scribe says *de te fabula narratur*, they arise in their wrath and protest against the wicked malice which pursues and vilifies their class. Shall the only perfect race of men in this sinful world be thus traduced? Never! Brethren, let us arise and slay this scribe, and cast his carcase unto the beasts of the field.

* * * * * *

When Pekoe Tips' papers came into my possession it seemed to me that matter interesting not only to the general reader, but to the planter of the present day might be extracted from them. The manners and customs of those rough and ready days would, methought, contrast well with the sweetness and light of the life of the latter day planter. But alas! for blighted hopes and shattered aspirations: woe! for the blindness of my mental vision. Into what an abyss did I fall! I, whose pride it is to count amongst planters some of my best, truest, and noblest friends, I was said to have maligned the whole race, and even drawn down on them the suspicion and mistrust of our paternal Government, by a sketch of a "wet night" amongst some youngsters in a planter's bungalow thirty years ago! This is indeed black ingratitude: I withdraw: I apologize. No one ever got "tight" in Assam; spirituous liquor was utterly unknown there thirty years ago, and has only been recently introduced, *medicinally*. It is occasionally prescribed by doctors, for the prevailing fever of the country. The following little sketch written from my own memories of Assam thirty years ago, without any aid from Pekoe Tips' Diary—to whose crime-stained pages it forms a startling contrast—will, I am sure, be acknowledged by all old planters as strikingly true.

HARRY HOLDFAST'S HATFUL.

Many years ago, when tea-planting was profitable, when every shareholder got a dividend, and every manager a large commission, there was a good young man called Harry Holdfast, who had what is commonly called a hatful of money. He was a *very* good young man. He never played billiards; he didn't know the ace of spades from the jack of hearts; he was a Good Templar, a Rechabite; always wore flannel next his skin; and held a double-first-class Sunday School certificate. Above all, he never, never—not even "hardly ever"—but absolutely *never*, under any provocation, said a big, big D.

At school he had been a very good boy. He had a big cake given to him once for some preternaturally virtuous action and he gave it away presently to a poor blind man, without abstracting a solitary currant. It is alleged that the blind man opened his eyes on turning the corner; called Harry and his cake scornful names, and traded the cake off for sixpennorth of gin. But this does not detract from the nobleness of Harry's gift. Harry was sorely troubled by his hatful of money, which came to him as a legacy from a pious uncle, who, having watched Harry's career as a boy with admiration, very kindly died as Harry came of age, and left him the hatful.

After much consideration and consultation, Harry took ship to India, having heard that a splendid field for doing good awaited him there.

It is recorded of him that before they had been a week out, in the Bay of Biscay, he called the watch on deck to prayers just as a squall was coming up and the topgallant sails ought to have been taken in. The Captain so far forgot himself as to use naughty words when the topgallant masts were carried away; but Harry reproved him, seriously and firmly, showing him the error of his ways. Before they rounded the Cape, even the bo'sun's mate was cured of his wicked habit of profane swearing; changing his curt and peremptory method of conveying orders to the crew into "Gentlemen of the starboard watch, will you kindly step up the rattlines and take a reef in the fore-topsail. Jack! please oblige me by standing by the haulyards;" and so on.

Arrived in Calcutta, Harry proceeded to the house of Mr. Backemup, merchant and broker, afterwards so well known as the head of the large agency firm of Backemup, Foreclose and Sellem, to whom he had letters of introduction. This good man, hearing of Harry's good intentions, and his hatful of money, at a considerable sacrifice to himself procured him a number of shares in the Bor-Labh-ulaisi Tea Company, to give him local influence, and got him appointed manager of the concern at a salary of Rs. 500 a month. A poor fellow who had opened out the gardens and worked them up to what they were, was got rid of to make room for Harry. But then *he* used to swear sometimes ; he had got into a shocking habit of taking a pint of beer with his dinner ; and, once when a Kachari coolie threw a hoe at his head, he actually lost his temper and struck the poor, ignorant, benighted heathen ! Besides, he was that naughty boy Tommy, who, when *he* got a cake at school, greedily eat it all up himself, and was very ill in consequence. Harry was a sort of relation of Tommy's, the latter's father having been married to the former's step-sister's aunt's cousin by his uncle's first wife. The relationship was a little mixed, so they called Harry Tommy's uncle. This is really the origin of the vulgar phrase " Tommy make room for your uncle."

Harry laid in a stock of tracts, flannel waistcoats, and moral pocket handkerchiefs, and started for Assam in the *Progress*, the first trip she made after the cyclone. She was rather crowded, and Harry gave up his cabin to a family of sick coolies, who had been too ill to wash for a long period, and were passionately fond of smoking the *hubble-bubble*. This naturally made the other cabin passengers very fond of Harry. They liked him so much that they wanted the Captain to put him ashore to wait for the next steamer, in which he wouldn't be so crowded. So considerate of his comforts were they.

Arrived on the garden, Harry's first thought was to seek out the Kachari to whom Tommy had been so rude, intending to give him a tract, and to ask him up to the bungalow to dinner in order to explain the tract to him. He was very sorry to find the Kachari had left, and taken all the other Kacharis with him, so that the garden was rather short of labour. However, he visited the Bengalee lines, going from house to house, telling the people how good he was, and what nice things he would do for them. He distributed a number of tracts and pocket-handkerchiefs, and at length came to the flannel waistcoats. One day he was sitting meekly on a *charpoy* in one of the coolie huts, trying to induce a young woman who seemed to be somewhat scantily clothed to put a flannel waistcoat on; when an irate Bengalee rushed up, "jabbered" fiercely at him in some heathen tongue, and knocked him endways off the *charpoy*. When the *kerani mohurir* interpreted what the man said, Harry was very much grieved to find his conduct so misunderstood; his motives so mistrusted; indeed he was quite shocked!

Harry found the poor benighted coolies were working much too hard. He reduced the *neriks*; provided soup and milk for all who said they were weak or unwell; and always paid out full wages on pay day. The good creatures *would* have worked had they been well and strong, so they were clearly entitled to their wages. Harry got plenty of labour soon, but still his garden did not flourish. He used to assemble the coolies every evening; have prayers first; and then expound to them the Ideal, the Beautiful and the True. He would have got the Rev. Mr. Dowding to come and preach to them, but that philanthropic gentleman had not then come out to the country. He had the sirdars up to tea, and occasionally some of the coolies, the men, that is. After his first misadventure he was shy about inviting the women to the bungalow. But the jungle kept growing, and the flushes didn't, which naturally made Harry feel sad. Some of his neighbours suggested that he ought not to keep the coolies in whenever it rained, but he could not find it in his heart to send the poor creatures out in the wet; although he acknowledged he would have got more hoeing done if he had.

Harry soon found that his wicked predecessor, Tommy, had introduced much levity into the social life of the surrounding planters. Some of them had given up their evening family worship, and only had service on Sundays. One depraved man, demoralized by Tommy's beer, had got up a case of whisky and a pack of cards! But he was promptly sent to Coventry by all the planters, until Harry went over and talked him into a better frame of mind. He burnt the cards (he had drunk all the whisky, and couldn't get any more in the district) repented sincerely, and was solemnly received back into the community at a tea-party given at Harry's bungalow in honour of the occasion. Thus did Harry do good wherever he went. At the end of three years his garden had ceased to yield, but the coolies were numerous, well fed and happy. Harry's hatful was chiefly in the hands of Backemup, for the dividends had to be paid to the other confiding shareholders every year, and good Harry promptly sent the money to Backemup to do it. There is little doubt that Backemup would eventually have got the whole hatful, had Harry not come to an untimely end.

A general meeting of all the district had been called to organise a mission to Calcutta to convert shareholders and directors to the true theory of tea-planting; to prove to them that it was an industry intended solely for the benefit of the coolie, to promote his welfare, spiritual and worldly. The meeting was crowded. After a few hymns had been sung, Harry made a magnificent speech, insisting on further self-sacrifice, and lives of more rigid self-denial on the part of the planters, and pointing out that the craving for profits, dividends, etc., on the part of shareholders and directors was but an unholy seeking after filthy lucre. The speech was applauded to the echo; but when Harry sent the hat round to collect subscriptions to defray the cost of the mission, by a most curious coincidence every man there had left his purse at home on the piano. Harry's righteous wrath was roused; for the first time in his life he lost his temper, and called them all a "measly lot," or words to that effect. And now mark how, even with a good man like Harry, punishment swiftly follows on sin.

The wicked man formerly alluded to had recently managed to import another case of whisky, surreptitiously. Fearful of its being found in his bungalow, and his being again sent to Coventry, he drank it all up very quickly. Consequently he had, the last day or two, been rearing snakes in his boots, and was naturally a trifle irritable. He resented Harry's rude remark; promptly brained him with a big bamboo; and proceeded to go for the rest of the crowd, under the deplorable delusion that they were of the same species as his pet snakes. It was remarkable what a unanimous sentiment pervaded that meeting; every man suddenly remembered urgent business at home, and left at once.

The wicked man felt lonesome at first, but Harry groaned, so he finished him off; and, pleased with his little excitement, went home also. Harry's beloved coolies promptly looted the bungalow, and secured the balances of his valuables and money; and so ended Harry Holdfast and his hatful.

P. S.—Gentle reader, please excuse the appearance of the wicked man. It is necessary to have a "villain" in every story, according to the rules of composition. Besides, Harry was becoming oppressively virtuous, and I had to get rid of him somehow. So many catastrophes have been used up by the sensation-novel writers in disposing of their villains, that originality is difficult to attain. So I thought I would try letting the villain dispose of the hero. Poison, railway accident, shipwreck, fall over a precipice, fall off a horse, etc., etc., are all played out. The villain, in a fit of D. T. at a temperance meeting, braining the hero with a bamboo, is, I flatter myself, novel.

In the future chronicles of Tezbrusaugar, I will confine myself to ordinary men and women. These excessively virtuous people become insufferably tedious, and hard to work.

II.—AN ASSAULT CASE.

NED KEARNEY was certainly not in a good humour. He was not a bad-tempered fellow, as a rule, but just now he was not quite in so amiable a frame of mind that a child might play with him. He had just come back from Kalaporbot where Ribiera had been "hauling him over the coals" about short outturn and sundry other misdemeanours, and giving him confusing and contradictory orders about how and when to pluck. "Generally making an ass of himself, as superintendents usually do!" was Ned's reflection as he turned over matters in his mind on his long, hot and rather moist ride.

Starting from Kalaporbot in an unamiable frame of mind, his temper was not improved first by a shower which wet him through, and then by the hot August sun coming out and steaming him. An agony was added when he arrived at Partigarh and found Barnstable had gone out somewhere to an out-garden; that his servants had taken a holiday in the absence of their master; and that the old *kania* Kachari bungalow chokidar didn't know where the keys were, and was densely ignorant as to the whereabouts of the brandy bottle or the beer.

So Kearney after his 15 mile ride, had come on through the remaining 5 miles of forest which separated Partigarh from Sunkeri, his own garden, hungry and thirsty; getting more and more irritable as his tired pony stumbled over the tree-roots in the rough forest-path, or made frantic swishes with his tail and curious gyrations with his hind legs, whenever the *dáhns*, or huge flies, stung him, which was frequently. Occasionally a *dáhns* tapped Ned instead of the pony; on which Ned, not being a really good and pious young man like Harry Holdfast, said naughty swear words. At last he came out on the banks of the Sunkeri; and seeing the *már* (ferry boat) on the other bank, dismounted and yelled *ghatwâl!* GHATWAL!! **GHATWAL**!!! in a rapid *crescendo* up to *fortissimo*, fruitlessly for sometime. When the ferryman at last condescended to appear and poled his curious double craft across to him, Ned talked to him for awhile in such fluent Assamese that it was as well there was no one there who understood the language but themselves.

In short when Ned Kearney rode up to his own bungalow he was in a most unamiable and unenviable frame of mind.

Now, if the fates—and the *hazri mohurrir*—had been propitious, Ned would have jumped off his pony, poured a big glass of Bass bottled by Hibbert and Saunders into himself, lit his pipe, and peacefully awaited his breakfast of "Assam pheasant"; his usual good natured disposition coming rapidly to the surface as the refreshing and stimulating fluid filled and warmed up the vacuum which nature abhors, and the fumes of the soothing weed stole gently over his troubled spirits.

But Ned's evil genius was in the ascendant to-day. On his very threshhold misfortune awaited him, in the guise of a hulking big cooly squatting sulkily over his hoe, with the *hazri mohurrir* mounting guard.

"*Ki hol?*" (what's the matter) was Ned's gruff return to the *mohurrir's* lowly *salám*.

And the *mohurrir* commenced a long-winded history touching on the misdemeanours of the cooly before him: how he had not been out to work for two days, but been malingering round the hospital, though the native doctor stoutly maintained there was nothing the matter with him: how this morning the head *mohurrir* had insisted on his going out to the hoe, but found on going round that he had not done a stroke of work, while he further asserted that he *would* not, threatening to run away, and so on; so knowing his honor was to return that morning he had brought him in to be reasoned with, and punished as his Lordship saw fit.

All this did not tend to improve Ned's temper, as may be imagined.

"Isn't it that brute Narayan?" queried Ned of the *mohurrir;* adding, in English, as he dismounted and stood over the culprit,—"If it is, I'll give him fits! the beggar is always skulking."

"Yes," answered the *mohurrir.* "Get up!" said Ned, gently using the toe of his boot as a lever to raise the man, who had been sulkily squatting on the ground all this while, eyeing the *sahib* askance from under his brows, but not saluting him, or attempting to rise to his feet in respect.

"What's the matter with you? Why won't you work?" asked Kearney. "You're the most troublesome coolie on the garden: always the last at work but always the first in any row in the lines. Why haven't you done your hoeing the last three days?

The man growled something that sounded like "*bemar*" (sick).

"*Bemar* be damned!" shouted Ned, "The biggest and strongest man on the garden," he added, turning to the *mohurrir*, "*Nohoi no ki?*" (Is it not so). "Now just you turn to and hoe me 20 nals of that ground across the road there; and if it isn't done by sundown you look out;" and Ned raised the light cane he carried as a riding whip, shook it threateningly near the man's ears, and was turning away "on thoughts of beer and bliss intent."

As Kearney shook his cane, the man grasped the handle of his hoe, and half raised it, while a dangerous look flashed out of his eyes. Kearney caught the glance and the motion as he turned,—and quick as lightning, flashed his cane once—twice,— on the man's arm and then on his shoulder.

"Would you? you beggar!" he cried, and raised his hand for a good "stinger." With a yell, the man dropped his hoe and fled, bounding over the garden bamboo fence, and tearing down the road at a pace that was a sparkling commentary on his plea of *bemár*.

Ned looked after the "bounding blackie" for a moment, half inclined to give chase—for his blood was up; but thought better of it. Turning into his verandah and briefly ordering the *mohurrir* to catch him and bring him back, he got his long deferred drink at last. After a bath, a good breakfast, and a soul-soothing pipe, Ned felt sorry he had ordered Narayan to be brought up again. "I shan't know what to do with him when he comes" he soliloquised. "I've given the begger a couple of cuts, and I daresay he'll behave himself better in future." So when Narayan,—who had been promptly secured by a couple of tea *sirdars* as he fled down the road past the tea-house, was brought, Ned surprised and disgusted the *mohurrir* by talking to the man and pointing out what an ass he was making of himself, instead of giving him the balance of the caning he deserved. Ned flattered himself he had thoroughly impressed the man, and that he was going to be a good boy for the future. Imagine his disgust when the line chokidars, reporting in the evening, calmly remarked, " Narayan has deserted. " It spoilt Ned's after-dinner pipe completely.

Orders were at once given to have him searched for and caught again, and a smart line chokidar and a couple of old coolies were sent out on the hunt. Three days afterwards they returned without the runaway, but with the pleasant imformation that he had gone right into Tezbrusaugar to lay a complaint.

Now, in those days the Deputy Commissioner of Tezbrusaugar was an austere man, who had rather the reputation of being down on the brutal planter, and of fully believing the then dawning official theory that the planter's chief use of the cooly was to lick him at sight, and to torture him occasionally, on the principle of the inherent right of every true-born freeman to " lick his own nigger." Gloomily revolving in his mind the reputation of the D. C. in these matters, the feelings of Mr. Ned Kearney were by no means enviable. Naturally a very good tempered man,—and one who had never acquired the habit of " hammering the fellow " he happened to be displeased with, he was all the more disgusted with the state of affairs.

Narayan was not the first man he had ever hit on his garden. Job himself would lose his patience and his character if he were put to manage a tea garden. Ned was only a good tempered, naturally fair minded and humane man, averse to hitting a man who couldn't or wouldn't defend himself or hit back: but he was not an angel. The plumage would be uncomfortable in the climate of Tezbrusaugar. Hence, under the various and manifold aggravations of the coolie, he had once or twice before had occasion to smite and spare not; but he always felt rather "mean" after doing it. Now here he was, sure to be run in for assault, by the biggest scoundrel and most highly talented liar and skulker on his garden, before a man whose reputation was by no means encouraging.

His mind was not eased by a note received from a friend whose garden lay within four or five miles of the station, and who often went in there. Walton wrote as follows:—

"My dear Kearney,

"Why have you been letting your angry passions rise, and massacring inoffensive coolies? What *have* you been a-doing *of*? There is one of your Sunkeri coolies in the Tezbrusaugar hospital, a mass of weals and bruises, which he says you decorated him with, and old Gainsford swears he'll 'make an example of you.' I thought you didn't believe in thrashing coolies? but you must have made up arrears on this fellow, to judge from the state they say he is in. Drop in here on your way into jail, old fellow, and I'll give you the last decent breakfast you'll have for ninety days.

Gainsford has made up his mind to give you three months. He won't fine you.

"Yours sincerely,

"T. WALTON."

A myrmidon of the court—the typical Tezbrusaugar "bobby," with a red turban on his head and about two feet of white mud on his legs, arrived one day and placed a summons in Kearney's hands. Poor Ned's forebodings were realized. He was to appear on the 3rd September at the Court of the Deputy Commissioner of Tezbrusaugar to answer to a charge of grievous assault upon the person of Narayan coolie. He set his house in order: gave the head *mohurrir* general instructions how to carry on the work for a few days; wrote to Ribiera that he had been "run in" to Tezbrusaugar, and asked him to send his assistant over to take charge,—if he were "detained long." That was the polite way he clothed his apprehensions of a month or two's jail.

It was a weary, weary journey, 18 miles on elephant-back, to Walton's garden. There was a road some five miles from Sunkeri leading past Walton's to Tezbrusaugar; but to reach that road a huge *bhil* had to be crossed; and, at this time of year, an elephant was the only possible means of locomotion. So with a roll of bedding and a small portmanteau tied on to the *gaddi* behind him, Ned plunged into the *bhil* on his elephant; slopped and "sloshed" through the mud and water occasionally popping into unexpected deep holes which almost wet the *gaddi*—for five miles; and then plodded slowly and heavily along 13 more miles till the Kakojan bungalow hove in sight. Of all the wearying journeys possible, on elephant through *bhils* and over bad roads during the rains is about the worst.

Walton was waiting breakfast for him.

"Have a peg," was his first salutation; but Kearney elected his favourite Bass, not being much of a hand at "pegs."

"You don't look so 'skeard' and dismayed as I expected you would," said Walton, as they sat down to breakfast. "Tell us all about it now, why did you go for this fellow so unmercifully?"

"I don't know what you call unmercifully, Walton; I only gave him a couple of cuts with my riding cane. The beggar bolted, or I *would* have given him more, I daresay, for he had lifted his hoe at me, and I was tired and hungry, and in a devil of a rage altogether."

"Come, come now, old man! don't take me for Gainsford," said Walton. "Have another glass of beer, and make a clean breast of it. Neither I nor Jones will give evidence against you;—will we, youug 'un?" he added, turning to his rosy-cheeked new assistant fresh out from home, to whom the cooly and the planter,—and their ways,—were as yet alike mysteries.

"It's a fact, I assure you, Walton," replied Ned, seriously; "a solemn, frozen fact. I only hit the fellow two cuts." And he proceeded to tell them the whole story as narrated above.

"But the man is just pulp, I hear," cried Walton, when the narrative was concluded. "He couldn't have had another hiding from your chokidar I suppose. Do you think so?"

"No. I saw the fellow in the evening, and he hadn't a mark on him. I can't understand it at all."

"What are you going to say to Gainsford?" queried Walton.

"What *can* I say?" said Ned. "I hit the fellow, and I must acknowledge I did; but I can swear I didn't make him the mass of bruises and weals you describe."

"Gainsford will 'jug' you as sure as fate, Kearney. Can't you swear you *didn't* hammer the man? If you admit one cut, Gainsford will credit you with the balance, and you know what a brute he is for taking a chance against a planter. If it were the Sibpur D. C. now, you'd be all right; *he* is a good sort, with no prejudices either way, for black or white. But the Lord help the 'interloper' who is delivered fairly into Gainsford's hands, as you seem to be this voyage!" And Walton hid his sympathizing face in his beer-mug, and then shook his head dolefully at Ned, after his drink.

"It can't be helped. I hit the fellow, and I must own up and take the consequences, I suppose. But how on earth he managed to come by all the bruises and weals you say he shows is a dark and dismal mystery to me."

"Well, let us be off into the station, Kearney, and see what's the news. I'll ride in with you, and if we don't find old Johnson, or the Doctor, we'll put up at the dâk bungalow for the night."

"Thanks awfully, Walton. I'm delighted you are coming in with me. I rather dreaded a moping evening in the dâk bungalow, all alone. I don't know any of the station people, you see. A fellow can only come across that beastly *bhil* for such little luxuries as a case in court. You'll have to lend me a pony though. I've only brought the old elephant; I'll take her along too, as I want to buy some stores in the basar to take back, if I find I am likely to want them, after my interview with Gainsford."

And Ned smiled a rueful sort of smile.

On their way in, close to Tezbrusaugar, they were overtaken by a horseman, riding furiously. As he pulled up behind them on the narrow road, they recognized the Doctor.

"Hallo! Walton; going into the station again! Shall have to report you to your agents, my friend; off your garden in this way. Who's that ahead of you? Ned Kearney, by Jove! Well you're just the other way—*never* in the station, so we'll strike an average and let the pair of you off this time." And the Doctor laughed a cheery laugh and ranged up alongside of Walton. "Gimmee a light, old man, and a fill of 'baccy,' like a Christian. I've soaked my matches and got a pouch full of water, swimming that abominable Kulni an hour back."

Walton handed him out the desired luxuries, and Dr. Green filled a short black pipe and puffed out a cloud of smoke with a sigh of satisfaction; his pony, evidently quite accustomed to the proceeding, jogging along contentedly with the reins over his neck as the Doctor filled and lit up.

"You look rather moist, Doctor," said Ned, glancing back at Green's wet breeches and soaked boots.

"Well, I *am* damp. The rivers in Tezbrusaugar are a little wet during the rains. What are *you* doing so far from your jungle home? Any new attraction in the station to drag you from the alluring process of making rupee averages?"

"Oh! I'm in on—on a little business, Doctor, and Walton's just come along for company."

"Trust him for any excuse to ride into Tezbrusaugar! But what's going on? I've been away up inspecting a lot of those gardens under the hills for the last week. But come along: you can tell me all about it after dinner. You'll come and stop with me to-night, of course."

"We were thinking of going to the dâk bungalow," commenced Ned, "but"—

"But you'll do no such stupid thing," cut in theDoctor. "You'll just do as you're told, and come along with me. Mrs. Green will hang you over a clothes' horse somewhere for the night; and I've just got a new cask of the real genuine stuff up. We'll tap him to-night, boys; we'll tap him." And away he cantered, leading the way to his well-known hospitable bungalow.

It was a change for Ned from the rough life he had been leading for some time, that evening at the Doctor's. Mrs. Green was in the verandah looking out for the return of her wandering husband, who was always flying about the district wherever sickness or duty called him. The arrival of two unexpected guests did not put her out in the least. Ned, as he changed his dress in the neat little room assigned to him, and when he came out to the prettily furnished drawing-room, and found two charming little children playing on the neat Calcutta mat,—quite ready to make friends and play with him too,—realized that there was a phase of life in Tezbrusangar more like "home" than he had deemed possible. Presently Walton strolled in; then the Doctor, followed by a bottle recently extracted from that cask before mentioned. A peg before dinner of the "real genuine stuff" threw an extra glow of cosiness and comfort over the snowy cloth and glittering plate and glass on a table such as Ned had not sat down to for many a long day. Mrs. Green was a homely pleasant little lady, and speedily made him feel as if he had known her for years. After dinner, while she amused herself with dreamy soft music on the piano in the next room, and they puffed a cloud over the dining table and another glass of the "real genuine," Ned's story and sad forebodings were told.

The Doctor grunted over the recital of the details of the assault, and derided Kearney's evident shamefacedness about having struck the man at all.

"You needn't be so squeamish about hitting a man who cheeks you, Kearney. I've seen old Gainsford himself give a man as good a hiding as any brutal planter amongst you all! Eh! man; the old Adam is strong even in the elect. Neither Haileybury nor competitive examinations ever took the 'punch-your-head for cheek' instinct out of a man!"

Dr. Green puffed violently for a few minutes, and then added: "I've a bit of consolation for you; and I've a theory. The first is, Gainsford has been suddenly called out of the station, my native doctor told me just now; so the old Sudder Amin will hear your case. And the other is,—well, I'll tell you in the morning, after I've paid your friend Narayan a visit in the hospital. The native doctor has given me a hint about *him* too. Come away and have some music. I hear you sing like a nightingale, Kearney: come, tune up and be joyful! I'll pull you through and keep you out of jail this journey." The doctor's cheery manner and hopeful view of the case brightened Ned Kearney up, and allowed him to feel more freely the delights of civilized music, to which he had been long a stranger. Mrs. Green not only had some of his songs, but some duets which they tried over together; and presently, Walton, developing a tendency to hum the airs they were singing, was pressed into service, and a trio or two hunted up from amongst the music, to which he contributed a melodious bass. The doctor's remark during a temporary lull, "Your throats must be getting dry; come away and wet your whistles," drew their attention to the lateness of the hour; and to the fact that it was time all good people were in bed. Ned lay awake long that night. Memories of home were surging up in his mind; the old songs had brought back the old scenes in which they had last been sung. He wished he lived nearer the station, or that some of the fellows down in his neighbourhood were married. Life in Tezbrusaugar would be worth living with this sort of evening in store for a man occasionally, instead of the solitary, cheerless, shanty of a place he lived in, with only an occasional visit from a neighbouring hermit, and a flat, stale and unprofitable conversation on the everlasting "shop."

Next morning, by eleven, Kearney duly put in an an appearance at *kacherri*, and was much more civilly received by the Sudder Amin than he would have been by the dreaded Gainsford. The Sudder Amin was a fine specimen of "the good old native gentleman," unspoiled by contact with the worst phases of Western civilization. He was not a B. A., had not even passed his "First Arts;" nor did he wear patent leather shoes. But he knew and did his work honestly and well; and was liked and respected by both Europeans and natives throughout the Tezbru-saugur sub-division.

Ned was placed on his oath and asked a few pointed questions as to the assualt, to which he replied plainly and straightforwardly stating the circumstances exactly as they occurred. The Sudder Amin pointed out the man's state, showing marks of a thrashing much more severe than what was admitted; and while acknowledging the evident candour and straightfor-wardness of Kearney's statement, said he must have further evidence.

"Have you brought in the *hazri mohurrir?*" he enquired. Now this is just what Kearney, in the innocence of his heart, and the sublime but misplaced confidence in the omnipotence of an Englishman's word—let alone his oath—had not thought of doing; and so he said.

"But here we have the man's deposition that you beat him most severely: he brings no witnesses either; but his wounds are so severe that he cannot even come into court," said the Sudder Amin.

"Can't he just!" called out a voice at the door; and in marched Dr. Green pushing the battered and bruised Narayan in front of him. "He's a painted fraud, this chap; no more bruised than I am—so you're all right this time Kearney, my boy!" and the doctor slapped him triumphantly on the shoulder.

"This is rather irregular, Dr. Green," remarked the Sudder Amin quietly; "but if you have evidence to give in the case it shall be taken properly."

And so it was. Mr. Narayan, who was practically unhurt by Kearney's cuts, to have his revenge, had availed himself of the botanical knowledge of a friend in the lines; and, the night he bolted, had carefully striped himself with the juice of some jungle plant pointed out to him. This had the effect of producing, with little or no pain, all the appearance of livid weals and bruises. Thus decorated, he made a most effective appearance at the Tezbrusaugar *thanna;* and after pouring out his woes there, took up a comfortable residence in hospital. The native doctor had "spotted the plant" literally and figuratively, almost at once; but for fear of the police, for whom Narayan had provided a beautiful "case," kept quiet, till the return of his superior officer, Dr. Green, from the district. Green saw the man in hospital that morning, agreed fully with his subordinate's diagnosis of the case, and promptly informed the interesting patient that he was found out, that the game was up, and he had better throw up his hand. He had just got him, very sulky and unwilling, to come along to court: "and there he is, the beast! and a pretty picture he has made of him self," said Green, winding up his evidence with a dramatic point at Narayan, as he stood, hands joined and with a dejected air, looking anything but "a pretty picture."

Ned was promptly acquitted, the Sudder Amin letting him off without even a nominal fine for the admitted assault, in consideration of the provocation, and the subsequent exaggerated charge. Narayan's residence was changed from the hospital to the jail for a month, for bringing a false charge. A few new friends made, and a couple of pleasant days and cheerful musical evenings passed, with a determination to come into the station as often as he conveniently could, were the only consequences to Ned Kearney of his first and only assault case.

III.—AN ORPHAN IN TROUBLE.

"COME over sharp, he writes, does he? And how the deuce does he expect I am 'coming over sharp,' when my only pony has got such a sore back I daren't put a saddle on him."

And Ned Kearney jumped up from the broken cane chair he had been reclining in, threw a letter he had been reading, angrily away, and commenced striding up and down the little verandah of the shanty he lived in, which was dignified by the name of his bungalow.

"I suppose I must just *walk* over! A lovely idea, at this time of year. Wouldn't mind it in the cold weather; but now, with the wet jungle miles over head, and hungry leeches dropping down the back of your neck in swarms! Oh! Lord;" and Ned shuddered at the idea.

"Let's see what the young 'un says;" and he picked up the letter again from where he had flung it. "'Mrs. Ledyard very ill—baby only two days old—Ledyard awfully queer—don't know what to do—come over sharp, for Heaven's sake and help through the trouble.' All very well, Mr. J ones," went on Ned, once more throwing the letter down. "But Ledyard is my boss as well as yours, and may want to know why I'm off my garden without leave if I do go. And a lovely reward of virtue *that* would be, after walking across to help *you* out of an imaginary hole. Besides, what can I do when I get there? I don't know much more about a baby than Jones does. Confound babies! Why does Mrs. Ledyard go and have babies in this God-forsaken place, fifty miles from the station, and the floods out. I suppose I'd better go over and see what's up, or Jones will get hysterics."

Ned questioned the man who had brought him the letter.

It turned out he had been sent yesterday afternoon, and should have come in last evening. Of course the coolie had preferred to remain the night in his house, and to start next morning. So a day was lost. Anyhow all the more reason for Ned to hurry across, if he could do any good by going.

Kearney had moved since we last heard of him. Ribiera was gone, and a new Superintendent reigned at Kalaporbot, while Kearney had been promoted to charge of an outlying division in the opposite direction. It was somewhat of an Irish promotion; but Ned was Irish, so that suited. Solari, where he now was, was a larger charge, comprising several small gardens; it was dignified by the name of a division. But it was an out-of-the-way place; not a soul near; and a dreadful shanty, as before indicated, for a bungalow. This was rough on Ned; after having made himself fairly comfortable at Sunkeri, building a new bungalow, and getting a few sticks of decent furniture together. The hut he now had was not fit to bring decent things into.

There is a popular superstition amongst planters against building a new bungalow: they say they are fated never to live in it. Fortunate indeed is he who, like Ned, is only transferred to another garden; the usual result of building a new bungalow is—the "sack." Like many popular superstitions, it is curious how many coincidences happen to verify it. Safe, staid, well-known old managers, who have been fixtures for years, and possess the complete confidence of their employers, occasionally build a new bungalow. It is funny how *they* go, too. Circumstances happen that a change of management is necessary. To build a new bungalow is beginning to be looked on as equivalent to sending in your resignation.

Ned had a very unpleasant walk across to Kalaparbot. Eight or ten miles through heavy wet jungle, over a wretched track which it would be misplaced courtesy to call a road, and with the certainty that dozens of leeches—besides the few which have obtruded themselves on your attention and been picked off—are battening on your wretched carcase, and will, most of them, leave nasty sores; this sort of walk is not pleasant as a rule. But the brutal planter in Tezbrusaugar gets used to these little luxuries.

Jones saw him coming, and met him at the foot of the little hill on which the bungalow was built. His face was very dismal.

"You're too late, Kearney!" was his greeting.

"What do you mean?" queried Ned.

"Poor Mrs. Ledyard's gone!"

"Good God! you don't mean to say she is *dead?*"

"Yes: died last night. I was wondering what on earth I should do about burying her; and if you would come soon. Ledyard is delirious, I think. You know he has been very seedy for some time with this wretched fever; down every other day with it. He had the hot stage on him last night; and his wife was dying.

And—I say, Kearney !—she called him from the next room where he was lying : 'Will! Will! come to me, quick !' I heard her, weak as her voice had been. And he got up, half dazed as he was with the fever, and went to her—and—oh ! my God ! Kearney, its awful ! He came out in a little while with the baby and gave it to me. 'Take the child Jones,' he said, half wild-like ; 'take and put it somewhere, poor little devil. Mother's gone and we will soon follow, I suppose.' And he put the baby in my arms and went and shut himself in the room again."

Jones broke down completely and drew his cuff across his eyes. He was very young ; had not quite grown out of schoolboy tricks yet, nor hardened his boy's heart by contact with sickness, suffering, and sorrow. Assam fever and death were alike new to him.

Kearney went up to the bungalow, Jones following, and found Ledyard lying in his own room, with raging fever on him, more than half delirious. He knew Kearney, called him by his name, but wandered terribly. He asked after the garden, Solari ; how much tea he had made that week. "Stay here a few days Kearney ; I'm awfully bad," he gasped out. "Mrs. Ledyard will make you comfortable." He paused, "No, no ! never again : dead, dead, dead !" And his hot head tossed from side to side on the pillow, keeping time to the monotonous repetition : "Never again ; dead, dead ! never again; dead, dead !"

The native doctor at Kalaporbot was—well, he was one of the old style of native doctors. They are not very brilliant now—some of them; but in those days they were a class, unique and marvellous in their ignorance, third or fourth rate compounders or dressers, mostly kicked out of a Calcutta hospital in disgrace. They were good enough for tea gardens. But there were medicines in an almirah; and young Jones, whose destination had been medicine at first, before he was sent out to make a rapid fortune in tea, knew a little more of their use than the native doctor. So between them, they gave Ledyard a diaphoretic mixture, which gave him a sweat, and cooled him down. Then they proceeded, after the manner of the period, to administer huge doses of quinine.

A rude coffin had been made by the tea-box cooly-carpenters, and a grave dug among the tea at the foot of the hill. The two boys—for Kearney was little more than a boy—debated whether they should ask Ledyard what to do, or act without him. He was quiet now and seemed asleep. If they roused him, there was no certainty that he would talk sensibly to them. Ned had written off to Tezbrusaugar, but the man could not get there under two days at utmost speed. It was no use waiting.

Women from the coolie lines—procured with difficulty from the lowest caste—had done all that was necessary before Kearney came. The two young fellows reverently laid the body in the coffin, carried it, with the help of a couple of old servants of Ledyard's, down the hill; and Kearney, in a voice which he somehow could not command, read the magnificent service of the Church over the grave, Jones utterly unable to make a single response, from the lump in his throat. It was a characteristic ceremony; characteristic of the pioneers of Tezbrusaugar. Only a young wife, who, loving and trusting, followed her husband to the wilds. Far from home comforts; far from friends or companions of her own sex; far from a doctor; far from the knowledge and the aid which might have brought her through her troubles and prolonged her young life to the brighter days in store in the future. Never again to watch and wait for Will coming up the hill from the tea-house or the garden; never again to make his evenings bright and homelike in the bungalow so far from civilization. Never again; dead, dead!

* * * * * *

The baby was becoming a serious question. It had been in a miraculous sleep for ever so many hours, but it was wide awake now. Wide awake, and in dead earnest too, about what it wanted; probably, Jones and Kearney agreed, something to drink. It was making remarks at the top of its little voice; evidently objugatory and abusive remarks, scornful ones too. It wasn't old enough to stuff its little fists down its throat, which might have kept it quiet for a while. It could only yell, and that feebly, when you come to think of it; and make absurd grabs with its little mouth at anything that came near the lips. Jones tried it with some milk in a spoon; they knew milk was good for babies, so they got some off the breakfast table. Baby made for that spoon like an alligator, and very nearly choked itself. The result was alarming. Some better method must be hit on. Ned was thinking.

"I say, Jones," he said at last, hitting on a brilliant idea, "don't babies have bottles? How are they worked."

"Dashed if I know. Wish I did," growled Jones, as he tried to engineer another spoonful of milk into baby's mouth, gently. "This thing will get my arm down its throat presently. It must be awful hungry! Do kids always grab like this?" and he managed to get the tip of the spoon—with his finger as a check—into position. Baby promptly took hold and sucked away vigorously.

"I have it," said Ned, and he jumped up. Where can I get a bit of clean rag?" And away he went to Jones' room, returning presently with a sodawater bottle and the rag. The latter he twisted loosely into a sort of wick; poured some milk into the bottle; put the rag, wet with milk, in, and pushed the cork in loosely, to keep all safe.

"Now let's see how it works," and he took a pull himself at the rag. "First class, Jones! I ought to patent this. Keep the bottle tilted up, so as to let the milk run free. Here, give me the infant. Which is the right side up of the thing? What a bundle of clothes it is!" And he gathered the poor little thing up awkwardly from the chair where Jones had laid it—wrong-handed, of course; who ever saw a bachelor take a baby right? "Here you are, my boy!" he said, as he popped the rag into the little mouth. "Pull away, my hearty."

"It's a girl," said Jones, as he solemnly watched the experiment. "Gently does ," he added, as the baby nearly swallowed the rag, and choked again over an extra supply of milk. "You must get a sort of safety valve, or regulator, on to that machine of yours before you patent it."

"Judicious elevation, Jones; that's the secret. See how it works now!"

And the little thing closed its eyes, and steadied down to a long pull, a strong pull, and a pull altogether. Presently its hold loosened, and it slept. Kearney removed his "machine" carefully, and gently and tenderly laid the baby down again, patting it gently as it stirred in its sleep. Some instinct, born of handling the infant, seemed to come over him. His eyes filled with tears, as he stood looking at it.

"Jones, we must take care of this wee mite. God tempers the wind to the shorn lamb; so we'll keep it alive somehow. Poor Ledyard will be no help to us, I fear."

"Can't you get a nurse from the lines, Kearney?"

"I will get a woman to come and look after the poor little thing, dress it, and so on: but a nurse? No such luck! Lots of women with young babies who could nurse it, but their caste won't permit them. No use trying. They would see the poor little thing die before they would nurse it. You'll get awfully fond of 'caste' when you know all about it, Jones. No, we've got to rear this baby between us, young 'un; and we've neither of us much practice in that line. Got no babies at home? No married sisters, eh?"

But Jones was as innocent of the ways of babies as Kearney. Meanwhile a woman was sent for from the lines. A sirdar's wife, a respectable, clean-looking

North-West woman, volunteerd to be baby's ayah, having once officiated in that capacity before 'going in to tea,' she said. She had seen better days apparently. But she proved an acquisition, and evidently had been what she said. She improved Kearney's bottle by adding water in considerable proportions to the milk and a trifle of sugar. Kearney, noting this, pondered on the Scriptural question of strong meat for babes; and realized that even milk in its purity is too strong for young ones.

Poor Ledyard sank gradually. He was better the morning after the funeral, if it can be so called; clear headed, but very weak. He asked where she was buried; asked to see the child.

"Poor little Florence," he said, as he feebly stroked the little cheek. "Will you join us too, or will you stay behind, all alone! Ned! you'll take care of her. Florence, mind, if she lives; another Florence; I hope a happier one."

"But you'll pull round soon, Ledyard. You are better already; no fever today."

"No, no! I'm going too, Kearney. I hardly want to stay behind. Now she's gone, I haven't the pluck to make a fight for it. Help me up. I must write to her people while I can. You know her family are in Calcutta. They will send up some one for little Florence, if she lives!"

Ledyard wrote his letter, and also signed a sort of will which he got Kearney to write out for him, and a letter to the Calcutta agents. "You must take charge," he said. "You had better take over the cash and the books at once, while I can think. My bad day to-morrow, you know."

In was no use dissuading him. He got annoyed if told he could get better. Ned took over the cash and went through the books with the *keranni mohurrir* hurriedly. Ledyard seemed easier when it was done, and his letters sent off.

"Now I am ready to go," he said. "Leave me; I think I can sleep."

Jones and Kearney had a long talk that night over their pipes after dinner. They were bright young fellows, lively and even "larky" as a rule; but Mrs. Ledyard's death and Ledyard's illness—to say nothing of the responsibilty of the baby—weighed on them and sobered them. Kearney had known very little of Mrs. Ledyard; but Jones, living there with them as Ledyard's tea-house assistant, felt the death very much. She was such a quiet homely little woman; so wrapped up in and so fond of her big handsome husband; so kind, almost sisterly, to Jones himself. The Kalaporbot bungalow had been quite a home to the boy. He talked in a hushed voice of the pleasant evenings he had spent there. Ledyard busy with his sketch book or his plans—he was something of both an artist and engineer—full of designs for the first rude, rough, rolling-machine, never, alas! to be completed. Mrs. Ledyard with her work-basket on the table, stitching away at mysterious little garments, and putting in a pleasant word or two, as he discussed the rolling-machine or the current garden work with Jones. Such pleasant, homely evenings! so different from a solitary, miserable life at an out-garden.

"Never again; dead, dead!" seemed to float on the still night air outside, as they talked.

"My God! what's that?" cried Jones, as both sprang up and out into the verandah.

They heard it clearer now, monotonous and slow, a rythmic rueful refrain; "Never again; dead, dead."

"Good heavens! its Ledyard down there at the grave" said Ned, horror struck. "He must be off his head again."

There he was, sitting on the new earth, patting his hand on it, slowly, steadily; keeping time to his mournful refrain. Ned spoke to him quietly; got his hand; soothed him and coaxed him back to the bungalow, and into bed. He was blazing with fever again; it had come on without ague this time. Jones mixed a draught for him; Ned noticed his dismal look. "The type of fever is changing," he said. Jones really knew a little about medicine, but not much. They decided to sit up, watch and watch; with his old bearer there would be three of them, turnabout. So the night wore on. Baby woke, cried, and was duly comforted with the bottle. The woman and her husband had both agreed to sleep in the verandah of the bungalow, so she was at hand when wanted. Ledyard tossed and moaned, and tried once or twice to get up, but he was not violent, and could be soothed down again.

A couple of days passed and the dâkman returned from Tezbrusaugar at last. Dr. Green was out of the station far away somewhere. Mrs. Green had gone with him, the man said; otherwise baby might somehow have been sent to her motherly care. Well, they must manage with baby the best way they could; she was getting on all right so far, apparently. Ledyard seemed better too; he had had a very long spell, nearly forty-eight hours without remission, and was dreadfully weak; but had been free from fever since. He feebly longed for the river, now. "Put me on board a steamer," was his constant request. "I want to get on the river. I want to get away." The grave had an attraction for him which he wished to get away from; he spoke of it. "If I am here I seem dragged to it," he said. "If the fever comes on I shall go there again. If I had strength, I would go there now. Put me on the river. One Florence has gone. Give me a chance to live for the other." His mood had changed; he was not so despondent, he wished to live—for baby. So Ned arranged to take him to the ghat, if the fever kept off another day.

But steamers did not crowd the Brahmaputra in those early days, as now. Weeks and weeks passed without a steamer, very often; one up and one down a month was about the average. And Ned didn't like being away long from Kalaporbot; there were a lot of coolies out of agreement who were a long time making up their minds to stay on for another year, and these gentlemen wanted a lot of attention paid them. It would never do to leave them to young Jones, who hardly knew enough of the language to get on with daily work he might offend their delicate sensibilities in a moment, by accident, and they would walk off next day to take an agreement on some other garden. However, Ned got them all pretty well *kushi*; laid on the sirdars and *mohurrirs* to make things sweet for them generally, and decided he could let matters ripen for a few days. They would be ready to sign when he came back, after seeing Ledyard safe on board a steamer. Luckily one was due down shortly.

It was a terrible business getting Ledyard down to the ghat at that time of year. The *bhils* were all full; the country flooded. There never was any road to that ghat worth mentioning in the cold weather even; in the rains, it is a succession of *bhils* and rivers. Kearney had to lay dâks of boats at the various deep places, and the extemporized litter was transferred from the coolies' shoulders to a *mar*, or double canoe, wherever the water got too deep for the coolies to wade; the dry land was all water too, as an Irishman would say, up to their knees. Kearney accompanied and superintended the procession on an elephant—and had to swim it in two or three places. They were all day doing the ten miles or so; but Ledyard kept up wonderfully, the idea of getting to the river seeming to sustain him.

At the ghat there was an old "flat" or barge, roofed in, on which Ned made Ledyard and himself fairly comfortable, screening in a sort of cabin with cloths. Of course they had brought down provisions and servants; and they settled down to wait for a steamer.

Meanwhile Jones was getting into trouble; so was the baby. Whether the latter got too much sugar in its milk, or milk in its water, or whether Ned's "machine" disagreed with it, cannot be certainly ascertained.

It got rampageous, howled dismally, and doubled up its little legs violently. The ayah said stomach-ache. Jones said any fool could see that; but what the deuce was to be done? If a cooly got a pain there, he generally gave him a couple of pills, or a table-spoonful of castor oil; but you can't give pills to a baby, and even oil he wasn't very sure of. So baby howled, and drank a great deal more than was good for it, like some other people in Tesbrusaugar, occasionally. Then Jones got into trouble himself. Those coolies wanted lifting over a hard place in the new arrangement being made; wanted more bonus, or blankets, or rum, or some other little delicacy which has to be administered in cases of renewal of agreement. Jones was afraid to undertake the responsibility of acceding to the extra demand, and tried to temporize. Then the coolies arose in their wrath and said, *dés jaiga*, after the lying manner of their kind, when they only meant to go to another garden, and not to their *dés*.

So Jones rushed a letter off to Kearney at the ghat.

"DEAR NED,

Up a tree again: two trees this time. Coolies all say they'll leave; and baby's got colic and does nothing but howl. What is to be done? Shall I give the coolies castor-oil, and baby a rupee more bonus and an extra bottle of rum? Hasn't that steamer come yet? Do try and come up sharp. How's Ledyard?

"Yours sincerely,

"T. JONES"

Ledyard was keeping fairly well; woefully weak and helpless, and slightly inclined to be light-headed; but

Jones' mixture seemed to be keeping the fever off. Kearney was afraid the coolies would clear out; some 40 to 50 old hands; it would be a terrible loss to the garden, and he was responsible. He spoke to Ledyard about it, who told him to go back at once.

"I'm all right, here", he said. "My servants will look after me, and the steamer can't be more than another day; then I'll have a doctor, and the change I want."

"But you are so weak," said Ned. "I'm afraid to leave you."

"You must go, it is your duty."

So he went. He saw that Ledyard had everything he could want; cautioned his two servants to watch by him night and day, and give him his medicine and his nourishment regularly; left a letter for the Captain of the steamer; and bidding Ledyard keep up heart, bade him farewell, with great anxiety, but with hope for the speedy arrival of the steamer. Ledyard was very, very weak, and seemed to lose strength instead of gaining; but the steamer *must* be down in a day or two.

Arrived at the garden Kearney managed, with some trouble and a few judicious "tips" to the malcontents, to soothe the coolies' ruffled feelings; and, striking while the iron was hot, got them all to sign agreements that very evening. There was a considerable consumption of rum that night in the lines, and sundry very sore heads next morning. The distribution of the rum to the coolies gave Ned a happy thought about baby Baby was still curling up its little legs and making nasty remarks at intervals, notwithstanding the extraordinary positions the ayah put it into, and the vigorous way she slapped its back and rubbed its front, alternately.

"Let baby have a drink too," said Ned as the result of his happy thought. "Brandy is good for you and me, Jones; it warms up *our* 'tummys.' A little will warm baby up too.'

"Capital," said Jones; "not too strong though. Water it well, like the milk; and I'll try the spoon trick again."

The Lord tempers the wind to the shorn lamb, as Ned before observed. They gave that week-old baby a teaspoonful of brandy and water, and little Florence took it down gratefully and cooed satisfaction. Surely a Tezbrusaugar baby indeed, this; to the manner born. Dill-water is not strong enough for the climate. And Florence went to sleep after it, too, and made no more nasty remarks.

Ned remained at Kalaporbot next day; he wanted the rum to work off before he went down to the ghat again. But he sent a note down to Ledyard, asking him if he wanted anything, and telling him the good news about baby and the coolies. Poor Ledyard never read that note. He was dead before the man got there that afternoon, twenty-four hours after Kearney left him. The up-steamer came into the ghat that evening, landing Barnstable there, who had beeen down to Calcutta on a business trip; the down steamer was aground miles up the river; so poor Ledyard had a better attended funeral than his wife, whom he so soon followed, as he thought he would. The Captain of the steamer read the service over him; officers and passengers all stood round the shallow grave scratched in the sandy *char*. It could not be dug deep, for the water was close to the surface; and it was but a temporary resting place, after all; for the river, ever changing its course, cut away the whole *char* soon after.

Who knows how he died? He was sinking for days, and the fatigue and exposure of the journey to the ghat must have hurried the end. Alone, and untended but by a couple of hireling natives—whose sympathies, God knows, are far enough from us in our health and strength—who knows what sad thoughts, what vain desires and longings, what last ideas, passed through that fever-stricken and enfeebled brain. Never again to work, to command; never again to plan and contrive. Never again; dead, dead! Only one of the many victims that the opening out of a new country claims. Only a brutal planter. Only one of the dozens and scores who have died to make Assam what it is now. Those who know what it was thirty years ago, know what the noble work of those who have lived—and died—in it, has made it.

And baby? Baby Florence flourished under her curious surroundings; waxed fat and kicked under the influence of Kearney's "machine" and occasional brandy and water; till a grand *dhai*, accompanied by a gorgeous and trusted servitor of Mrs. Ledyard's family, arrived from Calcutta, took possession of the orphan and her parents' effects, and bore them away. The little thing had wound herself round the hearts of her foster parents, so to speak, and the parting was sad. Ned Kearney often wondered if he would ever meet Florence Ledyard again, a bonnie winsome lass, a happy wife, and mother. Perhaps he did. In the vernacular of Tezbrusaugar, *Ki jane? hobo pai!*

SEVENTY-NINE.

A CUP OF ASSAM TEA.

"THE cup that cheers, but not inebriates,"—as the diving William, or some other inspired gentleman once observed. In the days of my innocent childhood—alas! how long ago now—I remember reading how many various processes and how many different hands were employed to produce that common, useful, always wanted, and never-found-handy article, a pin. And so, in my maturer years, I think how another chapter might be incorporated into that interesting child's primer, giving an account of the many processes and different hands employed, before the washer-woman, the duchess, or the tea-total temperance man can enjoy their fragrant cup of steaming Pekoe-Souchong. The coolies that have to be imported (speaking of Assam tea); the jungle that has to be cleared; the seed that has to be sown,—half of it occasionally not coming up; the hoeing, pruning, plucking, rolling, drying, packing, and despatching, which tea in its various stages has to undergo,—an account of all these processes might fill, not a chapter, but a volume, nay, a whole library of primers; while a goodly sized appendix might be added on the question of coolie *versus* planter alone, not to mention other collateral subjects;—as to how many imported coolies are cruelly ill-treated (from the Exeter Hall point of view) and (from a matter-of-fact point of view) how many planters either lose patience, "lick a cheeky nigger," and get two years for it; or, on the other hand, keep on presenting the other cheek to be smitten in such a Christian-like manner that they eventually lose almost all manly spirit. But I feel such a task is of a magnitude beyond my humble powers, and so I propose confining myself to an account of a visit I paid to the birthplace of Assam tea, the adventures and misadventures which befell me on the journey, the changes I noticed in the ways and manners of tea and its production since I had last visited the country some 12 or 13 years before; and perhaps, when the runaway pen cannot be restrained, an occasional digression on the collateral subjects alluded to above.

So behold me starting from the Sealdah station one night after a farewell dinner, at which, in duly responding to various people who were drinking my health and good fortune, I fear I seriously though temporarily injured the former,—and bound for Goalundo to catch the good steamer *Traveller*, which was advertised to leave for Dibrugarh next morning without fail. I duly reached Goalundo after a considerable shaking in one of the nice easy carriages which the Eastern Bengal line occasionally treats its passengers to, and found the *Traveller* getting up steam at a most ferocious rate, if one might judge from the volumes of smoke issuing from her funnels. But it was much ado about nothing. I hurried myself and my belongings on board in a great state of mind lest I should be left behind; and then of course found I had the whole day before me to settle down in, make myself acquainted with the novelty of my surroundings, admire the picturesque view of the sandy bank and grass huts on shore, and stare at and be stared at by my fellow passengers, till we scraped a mutual acquaintance. As a matter of fact, the steamer lay at the *ghât* all day, and did not leave till next morning.

Things were a little dull and monotonous at first; but it was amusing after a while to watch one passenger after another go up to the Captain and ask him when we were going to start; and to see the Captain,—after saying he did not know,—retire to the side rail and relieve his feeling in jerks of muttered profanity. He wanted to be off as much as we did, but their lordships, Messieurs the coolies, were not prepared to come on board. So the coals had to be burnt, the passengers to wait patiently, and the Captain to rack his brains inventing new oaths suitable to the occasion, until the colored gentlemen had been warranted sound in wind and limb, and as having had a good cooked meal from the depôt, before they were placed on board and handed over to the charge of the doctor on the steamer.

But they came on board at last, some two or three hundred strong,—men, women, and children; yellow, brown, and black; and a curious sight they afforded us. Some of us of the sterner sex of the passengers went aft to see them settle down on the after deck of the steamer; and again a little later to see the menagerie fed. For they were but poor, weak, frail mortals, and must have another "cooked meal" on board the steamer under the surveillance of depôt, embarkation, and steamer authorities combined, to see that change of scene and air had not taken away their appetites. The huge iron cauldrons full of boiled rice and *dál*, each cauldron taking two stout men to lift; the frantic scrambling to get first help; the dodging of some of the more knowing ones, especially growing children, who, having swallowed one allowance and licked their tin plates clean, adroitly changed their places in the line, or slipped down to the other end of it to "double the Cape" as sailors say; the combination of a superabundance of very dirty garments on some of the "north-west" coolies, with the scantiness of clothing and freedom from restraint (not to say decency) amongst the "junglies;" and, above all, the pervading smell of coolie—a scent never to be forgotten by the initiated—mingled with the fumes of the hot food, all combined to take away my appetite, I must confess. Sundry attempts to "fill the void" with such seductive drinks as the steamer's butler could produce, were necessary ere the tone of my stomach was properly restored. The other gentlemen I observed were somewhat similarly affected but everything works for the best in this world. It resulted in our shaking down into the intimacy with each other so conducive to a pleasant passage, while we were discussing the merits of various kinds of coolies (and refreshing drinks,) and purifying the atmosphere with tobacco in different forms.

In the course of conversation I gleaned several facts about coolies, and contractors' imported *versus* free and sirdari labour, which struck me considerably. One or two of my fellow passengers were old tea-planters, men of sound sense, good general information, and mature judgment, as many planters are, of course; and so I think my opinions on the coolie question are well founded, and not based on one-sided special pleading; especially as I had ample opportunity afterwards of verifying the ideas I had formed on the subject, from seeing how coolies generally were treated on several different tea gardens, and how the different classes of coolies adapted themselves to their novel surroundings. I did not then wander over moro than a small part of Assam, but I saw coolies on a good many gardens under various sorts of planters as managers. *Ex pede Herculem*, and on parallel reasoning I think I have a right to form an opinion on the matter, which, I have no doubt, will come out in the course of my scribbling. But I do not wish to sermonize; so I will forbear my learned remarks on the Emigration Act as long as I can. They are sure to be learned ones, as I know little or nothing about the Act, and therefore approach it with an unbiassed mind.

But *revenons à nos moutons* (a very ancient quotation I confess, but I am aching to air my ignorance of French, and it comes in just there handy), we *did* start from Goalundo at last, only a day late. Fortunately, the *Traveller was* a traveller, and ran up stream at a rate that defied the current and pooh-poohed the pretensions of the water to be rushing down from away west of Lhassa in Thibet, as the latest geographical discoveries in those regions would have us believe.

We reached Scrajganj by 4 P.M. on the first day, a very good run indeed. Here nothing would do for some of us but getting out one of the steamer's boats and endeavouring to distinguish ourselves in the eyes of the fairer portion of the passengers by frantic attempts to row. I was rather sweet on myself in this line, having once been stroke of a racing gig, but that was in the days of "auld lang syné." Consequently I succeeded in blistering my hands severely in my efforts to "feather my oar with skill and dexterity," the said oar being as long and heavy as the oar of a man-of-war's launch, and with as little *spring* in it as the piston rod of the steamer's engine. I can't say I enjoyed the boating much. In addition to blisters, it was otherwise marred. No. 3, just behind me, had a taste for shell-fish; and after catching several crabs, and digging me in the back occasionally in his efforts to get into stroke again, finally took a sudden and absorbing interest in the bottom of the boat, and disappeared over his thwart (backwards) to see what it was made of. His released oar, which he had been using "short" to ease the weight of it, took No. 2 in the chest and sent him back into the arms of the bow-oar; from which comfortable position No. 2 placidly contemplated the sky for a few moments, unheeding the cursory remarks of poor "bow," who was considerably mixed up with his own oar to begin with, and found the fag end of another which did not belong to him, under his chin, rather confusing.

But we reached the shore at last, and relieved our feelings by a stroll on *terra firma*, and by pelting the *pariah* dogs, who resented our intrusion by hideously howling and barking at us. We were finally routed by an old woman who came to the rescue of the dogs, and treated us to fluent Bengali, which we fortunately did not understand. Unable to bear up against her volubility, we retreated to the boat again; and were ignominiously rowed on board by the *lascars*, whom the captain had wisely placed in the boat, lest we should be found calmly and helplessly

"Floating, floating, far away."

Life on board a river steamer becomes almost as monotonous after a while, as life at sea; though I must acknowledge there is a little more variety of incident on the river than on the ocean. First thing in the morning, you are roused by the noise and bustle of getting under weigh. Unless you are an unusually sound sleeper, the rattle of the steam-winch heaving up the anchor, the yells of curious and unfamiliar nautical Hindustani, and the scream of the steam-whistle warning any stragglers on shore that we are off, are sure to wake you so thoroughly that it is useless to attempt to go to sleep again. Besides, unless your sex happens to be of the female persuasion, you ought to be sleeping out on deck to get the benefit of the cool fresh air all night; instead of being boxed up in a small bunk in a cabin with your nose up against a bulkhead that smells of paint, while the air is heavy with odours of all the occupants of the cabin since the steamer was built, with a whiff of last week's dinners from the saloon; and the mosquitoes sally forth from the corners where they hide themselves during the day, and sing triumphant pœans over your prostrate carcase. Sleeping on deck you have fresh air, no mosquitoes, and necessary early rising; which latter, as some one once said, is conducive to health. It is no use trying to "caulk it out," as they say at sea. If the noise and bustle of departure do not render you as thoroughly wide awake as the proverbial weasel, the rush of the fresh breeze along the decks as the vessel steams up stream, the constant passing to and fro of *lascars* and servants, and the noise of the coolies waking up to prepare themselves for some more "cooked meals," preclude all thoughts of prolonged snoozing. The necessity also lays upon you of getting up out of that, and being clothed and in your right mind, before any of the lady passengers turn out. There are horrible stories afloat of enthusiastic ladies who loved early rising and the cool morning breezes making unexpected appearances on the upper fore, deck by six o'clock, faultlessly arrayed in, charming morning costume; and the consequent frantic skedaddle of the lazy members of the male sex who were still recumbent; visions of *paijamas* of various patterns shooting madly into cabins or down the steps to the lower deck; and other dreadful incidents fraught with warning to the sluggard. Then there is the struggle for first bath. There is generally only one bath-room on board, and the early bird gets the bath (not the worm,) in the case. Finally, arrayed for the day in the garments of respectability, you re-appear on the upper fore-deck; and until breakfast time,—nine o'clock,—stroll up and down; read a book; make yourself agreeable to the ladies, who are now appearing one after the other; or hang over the rail to watch the water glide past, and listen to the monotonous but not unmusical cadence of the leadsman's "*sári do bám!*" which is usually chanted, musically speaking, on the fifth, rising at the "*do*" (or whatever other numeral may come in) to the sixth, and the "*bám*" sinking from fifth to third of the ordinary major scale.

Breakfast over, there are four mortal long hours to be got over before the next incident of the day, tiffin. How one eats on board! The river air, and the fact of eating being almost the only occupation, must, I suppose, account for the enormous consumption of food which goes on. No wonder the captains charge four rupees a day for sometimes rather inferior food; the quality may not be first class, but only look at the quantity which is devoured. Coffee and biscuits in the early morning; breakfast at nine; tiffin, a substantial meal of half a dozen side dishes and curry, &c., at one; dinner at seven to eight, after the steamer has anchored for the night; with tea or coffee and biscuits at four o'clock, lest exhausted nature should fail. Considering that one has no exercise except lounging up and down the decks, it is astonishing where the appetite comes from.

A favourite, though perhaps somewhat cruel, pastime, is to get out the various "shooting irons" possessed by the passengers; compare and discuss their merits; and try them on the hawks which hover about the vessel or perch on the masts of the flats; or on the alligators which lie sunning themselves on the sandbanks. Years ago, I heard a weird story of the passengers on the river steamers up the Ganges on the Allahabad line,—a line now long abandoned since the railway came into competition with it.* During the mutiny, when troops were being sent up-country by steamer, the young officers used to amuse themselves testing their rifles and guns as we did, but not on hawks and alligators. "Niggers" were considered fair game, when the blood was boiling in the veins of every white man at the stories of mutineer atrocities; and the *gowálas* (cowherds) and goatherds grazing their flocks and herds along the banks of holy mother Gunga, and who often appeared on the edge of the river to gaze at the *ághun bôt* passing, made splendid targets. I utterly refuse to believe a word of this, and merely give the story as told to me solemnly and soberly by an old river steamer Captain (long since dead) as a specimen of the way a monotonous life and the necessity of amusing the passengers with new and startling "yarns," acts on a lively imagination.

Of course, we commenced wasting ammunition before we had been more than a couple of days *en route*. Many and various were the weapons brought out, but the chief execution was done by a double-barrelled breech-loading gun on the hawks. The alligators got off rather cheaply. They were generally at long range, so it was difficult to hit them at all; while, if they were hit, they are such a scaly lot that it did not seem to trouble them much. Occasionally we could hear the crack of a bullet on them; but they would merely turn their heads enquiringly towards the place as if mentally saying "I wonder who's that knocking;" smile an extensive smile at the futility of attempting to get in there,

* Lately reopened again.

(what a very wide aud extensive smile an alligator has, by the way); and gently slide off the bank into the water with a derisive wag of the tail which was aggravating in the extreme. The skipper said he had sometimes seen them wink at the disappointed sportsmen; but skippers of river steamers are as a rule a curious class, and often say more than their prayers.

There was a little Winchester repeating rifle on board; a "Yankee notion," which was supposed to carry fifteen cartridges at once, and fire them off at intervals of about two seconds. The bore of the weapon, however, was so small, and the bullet so resembled a blue pill, that I could not but think it would take several of these pills to make a dose for an adult; and can almost credit what I heard on the subject of these rifles —another yarn of the skipper's. In one of those occasional differences of opinion in those vague localities "down South" or "out West," in which the usual arguments employed are bowie knives or manifold-shooters, one gentleman explained his ideas on the subject in question with a Colt's revolver, while the other gentleman replied with a Winchester repeater which he had by him at the time. The arguments went home on both sides, the former gentleman receiving all fifteen of the latter's reasons in his stomach; while *his* six propositions, dispersed all over his antagonist's person, had the effect of causing the latter to hunt up an undertaker and order his own funeral. But the fifteen blue pills, though a large dose, did not produce fatal effects, although they gave great inconvenience. According to the skipper, he met the gentleman a few days after, and was thus addressed :—"Guess they are an awful nuisance, them Winchester pills. They gev me a cramp in the stummick the day I took 'em, most like a circular saw going round in my inside; but that ain't the worst. Say, stranger, jes' you listen here!" and he shook himself, causing an audible rattle. "Hear that?" he queried. "Oh yes," said the skipper. "Wall now! I allow that's enough to make a man call his grandmother a skeesicks. Them pills keeps on a rattlin' in my innards when I'm walkin,' an' every fellow that passes hears 'em an' looks round, thinkin' I've kinder swallered my teeth, or got suthin' loose in my works inside!"

The Captain beamed smilingly at us all round after telling us the yarn, and then said he thought he'd go and have a drink. We heard him get after the *serang* a few minutes afterwards, so we knew he was all right, and it relieved our feelings. We had been afraid that he would never be able to fill the void satisfactorily after such a "corker" as the last. But he came up on deck again shortly, took a good look ahead for landmarks and bad water, and, finding all clear, bore down on a little group near the rail with a merry twinkle in his eye, evidently charged with another story. This presently was fired off with effect, to judge from the laughter, and the quiet dig in the ribs to which he treated Brown, who was next to him.

Another source of amusement open to us was watching the coolies. Feeding time in the menagerie was generally well attended, speculation going on meanwhile amongst the planters on board, as to whom such a batch of coolies were for, whether so and so was going in for *sardari* coolies now, or was still importing from the depôt, and so on. Comments on the *jât* or species were shrewd; this one was pointed out as a specimen of a man likely to do any amount of double *haæris*, and to thrive and grow rich through his trip to the tea districts; another was marked as a half and half sort of being, likely to get through his work if well managed and "judgmatically" treated; while a third was set down *ab initio* as a skulking loafer who would never do an honest day's work, spend most of his time in hospital, and finally die or abscond—a good riddance in either case.

The class most admired was, I found, the "junglies;" men from the Central Provinces, from Chota Nagpore,—Kols, Dangars, and such like. Those from some parts of Bengal, Cooch Behar, and thereabouts, were looked on with some favour; but what were termed "Nor-westers," were universally scouted. These are not men really from the North-West, or at least not from the upper part of those provinces, but mostly *luchas* and *badmáshis* of all sorts from Patna and Dinapore way.

But here is Dhubri, the first station in Assam, in sight.

Geography is a weak point of mine, but I think I am safe in saying that Dhubri is the westernmost station in Assam, on the Brahmaputra. At least, I am sure it was the first station in Assam the steamer *Traveller* touched at during the trip that I was on board of her. And here commenced the first of those shocks of surprise, which, occurring one after another in rapid succession throughout my sojourn in Assam, have, I fear, tended to weaken my powers of judgment, if not my intellect. This melancholy fact I must plead as an excuse for relating so many of the skipper's yarns, and not being able to sift truth from falsehood in those marvellous compounds. Many years ago there used to be a place called Bagwah, which one touched at before reaching Dhubri; but Bagwah now is no more. Probably, in the eccentricities of the river, it has been swallowed up, and now "calmly sleeps beneath the wave;" anyhow, it was not at home when we called. Nearing Dhubri, calling up reminiscences of it from the days before I grew through the hair on the top of my head, I formed wild projects of borrowing that dangerous weapon the Winchester repeater, and taking a turn in the adjacent jungle with a few coolies to bring home all the tigers and rhinoceri I shot. But when the steamer reached the place, I went to the captain. I said "This is a fraud! I shipped to go to Assam;—the land of jungle and elephants, the home of the tea planter and his tobacco-pipe; where long boots and brandy are the only evidences of civilization. I did not want to come to a place where there is a *Kacheri*, a Post Office, a Telegraph Office, and a submarine cable across the river for the steamer's anchor to get foul of; where there are bungalows with glass windows and flaming red curtains; good roads, with absolutely a pony phæton driving on them; and where the people are actually just coming out of church."

The captain took no notice of me, but called out

"*Arria!*" coupled with a remark about Chittagong pigs; which, as it was made in Hindustani, I considered could not be intended for me, but for the lascars who wouldn't *arria*, whatever that may be. I tried him again. "Captain, what place is this? Surely not Dhubri! evidently not Assam!" He looked round, and said, "Old man! you're not well. Go ashore, and see the clergyman." This finished me. I retired to the upper deck and sought spirituous consolation rather tqan spiritual; but the craving for the Assam of my youth was strong upon me, and I could not fill the void. I remembered the days of old, when land hastily cleared, and a lot of seed shoved in anyhow, was called a garden; when a few of these gardens were thrown into the market with a flaming prospectus, and a company formed to work the gold mine. Then "soldier, sailor, tinker, tailor, apothecary, ploughboy, gentleman, thief" as the child's patter has it, all rush ed into tea in one heterogenous mass. Dividends were paid out of capital to keep the shares up in the market till the originators of these fine schemes could sell out quietly; the hastily cleared gardens relapsed into jungle, or the untrained planters made nothing but red leaf. Finally the inevitable collapse came, and shoals of planters were thrown out of employ; many of them dependent on the kindness and charity of the steamer captains for a free passage back to civilization and Calcutta again. And, thinking over these things, I gradually became reconciled to the Assam of the present; with its good roads (here and there) and its dog-carts; its planters who actually wear collars and coats; who taste and even drink their own teas, and who make a bottle of brandy last more than a day or two. So, after another soda and something, I filled the void at last, and felt quite prepared for the advent of the *padre*, who presently came on board.

In the cool of the evening several of us went ashore for a stroll, and I was further alarmed by the sight of several ladies. Being naturally a bashful man, the shock was the more severe, as it was unexpected; so I hurriedly climbed up a little hill which was handy, and sat myself down on a small masonry platform on its summit to straighten out my ideas a little and get a bird's-eye view of Dhubri. I was puzzled at first to make out what I was sitting on; but came to the conclusion at length that it was the platform of a trigonometrical station; and so I found it was, on enquiry; one of those points on which surveyors put up a theodolite, and measure all kinds of extraordinary angles and sides by some mysterious process of their own.

From the hill I got a good view of the station; from the microscopic church on the left, built just on the bank of the river and apparently propped up by a rough scaffolding of bamboo to keep it from tumbling down on to the sands below, to the dâk bungalow, and another house or two on the right, with a back-ground of trees and jungle. There were two or three groups of people strolling about *kowa khána* "(eating the air)" amongst whom were several members of the fair sex; one isolated couple looking decidedly like an aggravated case of "spoons." My thoughts naturally went back to my first visit to Dhubri years ago. I used to be troubled with "spoons" then, but have recovered. The contrast was great. Then there was nothing but a couple of grass huts on the river's bank, in a small space just cleared of jungle; and on landing one's walks were rather confined and likely to prove exciting if prolonged into the jungle. I landed with a fellow passenger for whom my youthful mind had conceived a violent admiration, on account of the stories of various lands and adventures on the bounds of civilization in all directions which he could relate. He was an old gold digger, I think; attracted, like many others, to Assam, by the wonderful speculations in tea then going on; a huge, bluff, bushranger-looking sort of customer, with a red beard and a tender heart. We had not walked far along the path when a nasty looking black snake glided across it close to our feet. I jumped aside calling "snake," and he instantaneously put down his huge foot, cased in a long boot, on the reptile; which, strange to say, did not strike, but as he lifted his "beetle crusher" again, wriggled off into the grass. I shall never forgot the pathetic expression of his face as he turned and said, "Poor little thing! I hurt its tail!"

We took a lot more coolies on board at Dhubri, making nearly 600 souls on both steamer and flat in all; and after the usual delay to enable our new passengers to come on board comfortably after their "cooked meal," we steamed off for Goalpara.

Goalpara is supposed to be the chief town of Lower Assam, but it seems to have an unenviable reputation for unhealthiness, most of the officials who should reside there permanently, preferring to spend all the time they can at Dhubri.

I could see no particular reason for the unhealthiness of Goalpara. The European houses are chiefly built on the slopes of a fine hill, which rises to a height of about 300 or 400 feet above the river I should think; with a large flat top, which makes a capital lawn tennis ground, big enough indeed for a cricket match. There must be some reason, however, for the bad name the place has got; probably some swamps lying back from the river. The notoriously insanitary reputation of the place was made the occasion of one of those "sells" for which river steamer captains are celebrated, and which they laboriously work up to and lead unsuspecting passengers into. On one occasion a high official of Government was travelling up to Assam, intent on collecting statistics of all sorts, probably for incorporation into a gazetteer. He was given that way, and his appetite for facts was voracious. The skipper, of course, spotted him as a victim, and taking his opportunity when approaching Goalpara, remarked to the collector of statistics.

"Awful unhealthy place Goalpara,—dreadful!"

"Yes, so I have heard," answered the official. "Do you—ah—can you give me any idea of the cause?"

"No; but I can give you an idea of the death-rate."

"Ah!" and out came a note-book.

"Well, all I know is that in *one night* half the European population was swept away by an epidemic, to say nothing of the natives," said the captain.

"Good gracious! this is terrible—are you sure? Why this was never brought to the notice of Government, I can't imagine. The station ought to be abandoned. *Half* the European population! I must note this and report it. Are you certain of this?"

"Oh yes, you can mention my name as the authority;" and he turned away, paused a while and then added:

"You see, there were only two fellows living there last year, and one night one of them got cholera, and died."

The disgusted statistician closed his note-book with a snap and turned away; while the skipper went to stir up the man at the wheel, chuckling over how he had "fetched the old man," as he phrased it.

But the biter gets bit occasionally: even steamer captains can be taken in sometimes as the following will evince. Another special weakness of many river steamer men is bringing up things for sale; or, failing to sell them—they deal in more than one sort of sell, it will be seen—they get up a raffle. All sorts of things are brought up thus; guns, rifles, fishing rods, and patent gimcracks of all kinds. The captain in question just now, a noted joker too, the very Napoleon of "sellers"—had a nice little trap of some kind on board; dog-cart, bamboo-cart, or something of the sort, which he was anxious to dispose of. At one of the mukhs or landing places—a planter whom he knew well came on board; heard of the merits of the wonderful cart; said he wanted a light little conveyance badly; and down the pair went to the lower deck to view the article. The captain expatiated on the beauties of the vehicle; the planter examined it critically from all points of view, and chimed in seconds in the duet in its praises. The "old man" made sure he had sold that cart. "There's only one thing against it," said the planter at last, "or I'd buy it right off, I've only one horse, a little bit of a thing too; and I don't think it could drag that cart."

"Of course it could," cries the captain, eager to close the bargain, "the cart is as light as a feather!"

"My inmost soul is aching for that trap, captain," replied the planter, "but I'm sure my horse can't drag it; it's too heavy."

"Heavy be somethinged," said the skipper, waxing irate; "it's the lightest trap in creation! *Any* horse will drag it."

"Mine won't, I fear; it has other work already, mind."

"Don't care a pin! Come now; bet you a "chick" (Rs. 4) your horse can drag it, and we'll put it ashore now, and try it if you like," said the captain, now thoroughtly fetched at the imputations on the weight of his cart.

"I'll take your bet," said the imperturbable planter, "and you needn't trouble to get your cart ashore." He added after a while, "*My* horse is a clothes horse; I don't think it could drag that thing *very* far!"

The skipper had a severe attack of "cussin" for a while; but presently he "owned up" and ordered drinks round, telling his friend that he would have to get up rather early next time to catch him so sound asleep.

We reached Gauhati at last, anchoring at the upper *ghât* above the picturesque looking Peacock Island, with its temple peeping out from the dense foliage rising almost from the water's edge; and just below a small tea plantation, the first I had seen for many years. I immediately went ashore and wept over the nearest tea bush, of course; and was immensely relieved to find that my tears had washed off the "red spider" it was suffering from. I then had a walk round and returned on board, hot but happy (it was early in the afternoon), and watched the beauty and fashion of Gauhati displaying themselves on the Mall or esplanade, all the rest of the afternoon. Gauhati is the capital of Assam. I make no extra charge for geographical facts; even the above will be news to some. There is a regiment quartered here, of course in the unhealthiest site in the place, but soldiers should be hardy.*

And here my voyage must end; if I mention the particular Mukh I landed at I shall be accused of making personal remarks.

* * * * *

A high bank topped with tall grass, through which a couple of desolate looking huts were peeping; a small, decked, iron boat moored under the bank; a couple of miserable skeletons of carts, with iron wheels and a general air of dyspepsia on them; a solitary *himulu*, or cotton tree, with a damp, dejected looking crow on it, croaking out a dismal welcome, and a drizzle of fine rain. This was the cheerful prospect which lay before me the morning I landed on the

* The regiment has long since been removed.

banks of the Brahmaputra to make my way inland to my destination. The good steamer *Traveller* had travelled to some purpose, and was a couple of days ahead of her time; so there was neither elephant nor pony to meet me, as I had anticipated—not even a cow or a buffalo to ride; and I knew I had about twenty odd miles to travel. But there was no help for it; so, bundling my belongings on shore and telling my servant to sit on as much as he could of them to keep them dry, I bade my fellow passengers and the cheerful skipper farewell, and climbed up the bank to the huts to prospect the capabilities of the place. I must confess I felt somewhat like Robinson Crusoe, or Paddy on a "dissolute island,"—for a while; but the rain cleared off, the prospect and the sky brightened, and naturally so did I after a time. I found a godown *mohurrir* (clerk) and one or two Bengali coolies about the huts, besides some Assamese, or Miris perhaps. After a curious polyglot conversation in which the mangled remains of my Assamese (considerably rusty after 12 years' disuse) jarred and jangled with the *mohurrir's* attempts at Hindustani, and the curious gibberish of the Bengalis, a man turned up who addressed me in fluent up-country Urdu—apparently an old sepoy or policemen—and I felt relieved and happy once more. I was inclined to fall on his neck and weep, but he looked hardly clean enough for the purpose. However, with him as interpreter, I succeeded in procuring the use of one of the dyspeptic looking carts and getting a couple of bullocks hunted up from the jungle. Having been told that there was a dâk bungalow *(mirable dictu!)* only a couple of miles off, I started for it, leaving my baggage to follow; but rather doubtful as to the fact of the dâk bungalow's existence save in the fertile imagination of my Hindustani friend, as such a thing would have been a *lusus naturæ* in the good old days of Assam. It was there all right, however; a low rambling affair with *ekra* (reed) walls, thatched roof, and remarkably crooked posts, but not at all uncomfortable on the whole. And, better still, an elephant was there awaiting the steamer's arrival, and a note for me from the gentleman I was going to visit, with elaborate directions, as to my road, and the cheerful intelligence that a pony was coming also. The elephant had only just arrived, the steamer not being expected so soon; so I concluded to stay where I was for the day, and start early next morning. There was a cook, the inevitable fowl and something to drink, besides a few tattered books on a side-table; so I settled down. And when tired of trying to find missing pages in the books to get on with some story whose commencement had interested me, and of reading the curious remarks in the dâk bungalow book made by passing travellers, I fell back on trying to rub up my Assamese on the cook, and so spent my first day on Assam ground.

Next morning I started on the elephant, but the road being good, took to walking after a while; and after a few miles met the pony coming to meet me. The promised change in the method of progession was agreeable, but as I stooped to put on my spurs, the *syce* remarked I had better not encumber myself with them; and so I found on mounting. The pony just let me throw a leg over him, when he was off like an arrow and had covered half a mile before I was settled in my seat. Knowing Assam roads of old (as I thought), I tried hard to pull him in, but as he had a mouth of iron, and only a ligut snaffle bit, it was about as much use as bolting a door with a boiled carrot. I saw a bridge ahead and took another vigorous pull; but it was no good, so I just "let her rip," inwardly expecting a collapse. The pony shot over the bamboo matting which covered the bridge "like greased lightning through a gooseberry bush," and I breathed freely again.

An Assam bridge is a curious structure. Somtimes it is conspicuous by its absence, and then you dive down into a *jan* or ravine, splash through the mud and water at the bottom, (or stick in a quicksand perhaps) and climb up the steep bank on the other side. Sometimes it is covered with loose planks laid crosswise, which wobble under your pony's feet, and an occasional long nail sticks up to trip or lame him; sometimes it is covered with matting made from thick split bamboos; sometimes it is just a lot of bamboos laid longitudinally over which there ought to be earth, but there isn't; and sometimes it is like the Irishman's coat, just a lot of holes stuck together. I have crossed all kinds of bridges in my travels, from the magnificent railway bridges on the East Indian and the South Indian Railways, to the primitive rope *jula* of the Himalayas. But riding a pony which *wont* be held steady, haphazard over any kind of Assamese bridge that may occur in 20 miles of road, was a novel experience, and decidedly exciting. Driving over them, as I did on the second part of my journey, was even more lively. There are never any side rails; the bridge is often just a few inches wider then the cart, and the loose planks get up and buck under the wheels in a most exhilarating fashion. But I reached my destination all safe and sound at last. Planters everywhere are proverbially hospitable; the Assam planter is no exception to the rule; and there is no need to describe my reception, and how comfortable and thoroughly at home I was made at once; *cala va sans dire.* But I must describe two Assam bungalows at least, as they may be novelties to many readers; so I will select two which, allowing for the individual tastes and idiosyncrasies of the occupants, are fairly typical of the rest. The first style I may call the sternly practical order of architecture, the pure and unadulterated genuine Assam bungalow. The second is an innovation in many ways; the result as to exterior design, of improved ideas on the subject of health, convenience, and comfort, and as to interior arrangement and decoration, of the magic presence of the fair sex; for the Assam planter is a very much more married man than he used to be.

The first style of edifice is simple and unimposing; as to plan, it comprises a central room or hall with two other rooms, one on each side, opening out from it; a verandah running the length of the three rooms in front, and a similar verandah at the back, the two ends of which, however, are generelly enclosed as bathrooms or godowns. The central room has usually four huge posts, one at each corner—the main supports of the whole building—on which are laid the cross-beams supporting the king-posts for the ridge; there are four doors one in the centre of each wall, leading into the front and back verandahs and side-rooms respectively. There may be a couple of windows also, one on each side of the front door. The walls are simply double rows of *ekra* (reed), and are made by tying light bamboo slats, or *kámis*, horizontally from post to post, about a foot or two apart, vertically laying the reeds perpendicularly one on each side of the *kámis* (so that they enclose and hide them) and tying them on with long strips of cane, the correct thing being a kind of cross-tying which a lady would call a "herring-bone stitch." The openings and framework for doors and windows are made by leaving a hole in the reeds, of the size and shape needed, the edges being bound by a bamboo split so as to give a semi-circular section, which is tied on with the ever ready cane. The windows are "glazed" with a mesh of finely split bamboo; the door and window-shutters are mats, stiffened by bamboo *kámis* and bound round by split bamboos; and either swing from primitive bamboo and cane hinges on their upper edges, having to be propped up by a bamboo when open, or slide on a bamboo above, to one side of the opening, and again over it, when you wish to shut the door. The floor, a mud-pile raised a foot or so above the level of the ground, is covered with coarse matting of split bamboo; and the ceiling—well, there isn't any, generally.

And there is your bungalow complete. Nothing but a few posts, bamboos, cane, and grass; not a nail or a particle of iron, not a piece of string even, in the whole concern. Give an Assamese some posts and plenty of bamboos, grass, *ekra*, and *baint* (cane,) with an adze, a morticing chisel, and a *dau* (the heavy knife they use) and if he is worth anything he will turn out a complete bungalow with no other materials or tools.

The other bungalow, which I may style the composite order of Assam architecture, is a far more pretentious building. The framework of posts, beams, etc., is much the same, and the walls and roof, reed, bamboo, and grass, as before, but the plan is much more elaborate. First of all, the rooms are all raised on a *chang*—a *machan* as the Nor-Westers call it—to a height varying from 3 to 7 or 8 feet. This is done by planting short posts of the height required at regular intervals amongst the loftier ones which bear the frame work of the roof, laying beams across them, and planking them over; thus there is a smooth, wooden, raised floor through which the real posts of the building pass. The lower or ground floor as it may be termed, is generally left open; but sometimes a part is enclosed to serve as office, godown, store-room for factory-tools, garden implements, etc., and also to stow away your dog-cart and other odds and ends, under the first floor. The planked floor above is reached by wooden steps, more or less grand according to circumstances.

But, although the walls are generally reed, as in the other bungalow, there is a great difference in th. general appearance of things. First there will be a dining-room *and* a drawing-room, perhaps a small sitting-room or office besides; two or three bed-rooms, with dressing-rooms, and a fine open verandah as well. The walls are plastered with mud, and whitewashed over, (though occasional earthquakes crack the plastering considerably!) the smooth plank floor is covered with a nice Calcutta mat; the door and window frames are of neatly squared woodwork, and the doors and windows panelled and glazed; a white ceiling cloth stretched tightly overhead, purdahs to the bed-room doors, curtains, a carpet, a few pictures, and very probably a piano in the drawing-room; in short everything utterly unlike what an old stager like myself, revisiting former haunts, would expect. The first time I entered a bungalow of this class I nearly fainted! The shock was too much for my feelings, already agitated by the sight of steam engines in the tea-house and all kinds of mysterious rolling-machines. I recovered, however, on the prompt administration of an *iced* B. and S. (another innovation, ice machines!) and soon felt well enough to enquire into the changes in the mode of manufacture.

* * * * *

The origin of tea in India is, and I suppose ever will be, a disputed point. Some authorities assert that it was originally introduced from China, others that it is truly indigenous in India; and indeed some go so far as to allege that it is an exotic in China, introduced there from India. I must confess that from all I have read on the subject, I rather incline to the latter opinion myself, astounding as the idea may be to those who have always been accustomed to look upon China as the native home of tea, and the Indian article as an interloper in the market. The balance of proof in such arguments as I have come across is decidedly on the side of India as the original home of tea; perhaps, however, more cogent reasons may have been advanced in favour of China which I have not seen. For the amusement of those interested in the subject, I will briefly sum up the *pros* and *cons* on the subject from the China point of view.

To begin with, the botanical name, *Thea chinensis* evidently points to China as the native home of *Thea*, tea. It is known to have been cultivated in China ever since anything at all has been known about China. The members of a scientific committee deputed by Government to visit Assam in 1836, shortly after the discovery of so-called indigenous tea there, to enquire into the fact, gave their deliberate opinion that "it was probably artificially introduced from China." Mr. Samuel Baildon, whose little brochure "Tea in Assam," I have seen, ingeniously settles the question on the ground that the general Indian name for tea, *cha* is almost identical with the Chinese name for it, *tcha*; therefore tea *must* have come from China, *q. e. d.*

But the other side of the case has yet to be heard. The botanical name cannot be held as conclusive evidence. When that name was given, tea was only known as coming from China, and had not been heard of in India. But tea has never been seen or heard of in a *wild* state in China. That it has been cultivated and manufactured there from time immemorial must be allowed. On the other hand, it is known to grow wild in Assam, Cachar, Sylhet, and, for aught I know, in other parts of India. The scientific committee deputed to enquire into the facts connected with indigenous tea in Assam, although they gave their opinion that it must have been introduced from China, had very little reason to advance in support of their assertion, merely conjecturing that some tea seed *must* have been dropped somewhere from some caravan from China, and finding the soil and climate congenial, it grew and flourished.

The very fact of tea being found wild in India, and merely in a cultivated state in China, is a strong argument in favour of India as its home. Again, a Chinese legend assigns the introduction of tea into China to an Indian devotee, somewhere away back in the misty ages of mythological tradition. Mr. Baildon acknowledges that it is asserted that tea was grown and used in Assam long before China tea ever found its way there, yet he considers the fact of its being called *cha* a sufficient proof that it must have been introduced from China, notwithstanding this tradition, and the fact that it is found growing wild in the jungles in many places. I cannot make out where Mr. Baildon gets his Chinese word *tcha.* The Chinese language varies so from province to province, that men from Shanghai, coming round to Hong-Kong for the first time, fail to understand, or make themselves understood by, the people there ; hence a generic name for tea common to the whole of China is improbable. In Chinese Thibet alone I am aware of eight different names for tea, each for a different variety imported from a different province, and none in the remotest way resembling *tcha.* Here they are: *Dothang, Rikong, Galdan chioba, Koár chioba, Sirsio chioba,* (the *chioba* may perhaps be held to resemble *cha* slightly,) *Chung jung, jangja,* and *jangja-pari.* After all those "jaw breakers," I don't think Mr. Baildon's argument will hold water. Any one who has read an article on the tea plant by James H. Rainey in the *Asian* (to which I am indebted for a good deal of the foregoing) will surely have little doubt that India is the true home of tea.

Since the discovery of tea in a wild state in Assam in 1823 by Major R. Bruce, it has been found in Cachar, in Tipperah, in Sylhet, and has been planted and successfully cultivated in various parts of the Himalayas, from Darjeeling on the east to Kangra on the west. From these hills on the north to the Nilgherris—and even to Ceylon in the south—tea has spread itself, and is flourishing over almost the whole of India. Even if not a native of the country, it must be allowed to be a thriving and thoroughly naturalized colonist.

Government, as an abstract idea, gets abused a good deal for standing in the way of private enterprise in India, and perhaps the abuse is deserved to some extent; yet on the other hand Government has certainly initiated most of the great undertakings of the day. It is far beyond the province of the present papers to discuss how far Government really does interfere with and partly paralyse private enterprise; at a superficial glance there is undoubtedly a strong case against it. In no other country in the world can we find railways, canals, roads, and surveys made and carried on entirely by Government, by means of huge departments with enormously highly paid executive and supervising officials, and crowds of subordinates, from Assistants of all sorts down to the ubiquitous Bengali Baboo. This kind of thing is done elsewhere, under the orders of Government, perhaps, but by private enterprise, in the shape of large engineering firms, or reliable contractors. But private enterprise in India is a delicate plant somehow. The enervating influence of the climate seems to sap its energies at first, and it requires a good deal of coaxing and nursing to attain a sturdy self-reliant growth. Capital does not readily come forward for any project, no matter if the best financial or other authorities pronounce it a safe and paying speculation, without a Government guarantee of five per cent., or something of that kind. And so it must be acknowledged, growl as we may, that a great deal is due to our paternal Government for the initial experiments or preliminary guarantees which it so readily has undertaken or offered, in starting any new industry or enterprise. Tea, coffee, cinchona, and many other industries, are all indebted to its fostering care, putting aside the railway and irrigation questions.

The first tea gardens in Assam, of course, were Government ones; and as soon as it was found that tea would certainly pay, private enterprise nobly stepped forward and accepted the risk; not before. The first company was, I think, the one which is still about the best and most flourishing up to date, the

Assam Company; many others soon followed; share speculations naturally supervened; bubble companies, or at least companies on unsound bases, were got up; dividends were paid out of capital. Heavy Calcutta expenses, swell offices, gorgeous boards of directors, meeting as often as possible and drawing a gold mohur each director per meeting, and many other little trifles of a similarly economical and business-like character, soon combined to bring round the inevitable smash; and tea, which had soared to the skies and attracted men of all nations, tribes, and kindreds, (yours truly, *inter alia*) fell again, and great was the fall thereof.

But I did not propose writing a homily on vaulting ambition (or speculation) overleaping itself and going "ker-slap" on the other side, so I had better go on where I left off, after this long-winded digression.

The first thing that attracted my attention in the tea-house I first visited, was a lot of tea drying off on zinc sheets out in the sun. This was a novelty to me, but as it is not a very general practice, I shall merely note that it has its backers and its detractors, like almost every other process of manufacture. One drawback is, that you are not always sure of the sun. It rains *sometimes* in Assam. Some hold that the free exposure to the atmosphere weakens the tea; their opponents retort that the sun turns out better looking tea than the charcoal-fires; the little "flowery Pekoe" tips looking like bits of white floss-silk, while in charcoal fired tea they are generally somewhat yellow or orange. Again, the zinc sheets are supposed by some to give a metallic flavour to the tea; this may be obviated by a sheet of tea-cloth over the metal, which, however, causes considerable loss of solar radiation and drying power. In my poor opinion, if I may presume to give one, I should prefer a charcoal firing or a Sirocco.

But I may as well roughly sketch, for the benefit of such of my readers as are not planters, the old system of manufacture, craving pardon for any slips of memory from such as are old planters. Twelve years' pilgrimage in India, from the Deccan to the Himalayas, had made my reminiscences of tea very vague till I revisited the half-forgotten scenes again; and I fear I am a better judge of whiskey than of tea nowadays.

I may premise that tea is made of the leaves of the tea-bush, in India at least; elsewhere, rumour hath it tea is often made of sloe and various other leaves, so the piece of information above given is not so utterly gratuitous as it appears at first sight. The said tea leaves, after plucking from the bushes, had in former days to undergo eight processes before being weighed into store as "dry tea." Withering, first or green rolling, fermenting, panning, second rolling, second panning, third rolling, and firing or drying off; the latter process often extending far into the night, and giving the tea-house assistant a lively time of it, if he attended to his work properly, which he very seldom did. The tea *sirdars* had to look to it mostly; anything did for tea in those days, before brokers got so knowing, and Calcutta agents indulged in the luxury of professional tea tasters. The withering simply consisted in spreading the leaf out on the matted floor of the tea-house, thickly or thinly according as it was wet or dry—or perhaps on a *chang*—and leaving it till morning. The rolling, all done by hand, was commenced next morning, when the leaf was supposed to be flaccid and withered enough not to break, or "crackle" audibly when crushed in the hand, and was done at a *nerik* of about 20 seers per man. Often in the height of the season, when labour was short, the rolling was protracted all day, the men having to do "doubles," with the natural consequence of over-withered leaf, and the remaining processes hurried over and yet too long delayed. The fermenting was then, as now, various; the rolled leaf was packed lightly into a box, or piled up in a huge heap, or put up in smaller heaps, or spread loosely but thickly on a table. When fermented sufficiently, the panning commenced, in a large iron *karai* over a blazing wood fire; and after the rolling, "hot, all hot" from the *karai*, another panning and another rolling were gone through, and then the tea was taken off to be fired or dried. Little *chulas* in the mud floor, with a charcoal fire in each, over which large basket-work drums were placed, and on these drums, or *dhols* as they are called, flat circular basket-work trays on which the tea was spread, covered by other similar trays; this was the only drying apparatus.

With the introduction of rolling machines, the disuse of panning, and improved systems of firing, tea manufacture is a much quicker and less laborious process now than in former years; and, as a natural consequence, much more care can be and is given to the manufacture. The withered leaf is now merely rolled off in the machine, fermented, and dried or fired off in the sun, over charcoal, or in drying machines; and the tea-house work, even in the height of the season, should be over by nightfall. I will endeavour to note a few of the latest "wrinkles" in fermenting and firing—processes on which the quality of the tea entirely depends, provided that the leaf is decently plucked, in good time, and not allowed to stay too long on the bushes and get hard; and provided also that the rolling machine is a respectable one, and not worked too fast at the first putting in of a batch of leaf; a not uncommon error, which breaks up the leaf ruinously and never gives a nice "twist." Rolling machines have their little eccentricities too; driving bands part occasionally and "fetch" an unwary bystander; the engine gets up to tricks sometimes; and one curious rolling machine like an exaggerated mangle, into which you put the leaf in bags, has a knack of kicking out unexpectedly, bursting the bags, and scattering the leaf—and the coolies—to the four winds of heaven. But accidents will happen in the best regulated families.

The chief difference between the former system of tea manufacture and the present would, at a superficial glance, appear to be in two points only; the introduction of machinery, and the disuse of panning. A closer inspection of the matter, however, reveals something more. Though the number of processes through which the tea passes ere it is finally ready for packing have been diminished, yet far greater care is taken with the remaining operations, which are regulated with a nicety, and watched with an anxiety, almost entirely unknown and deemed unnecessary ten or fifteen years ago. In those happy careless days *anything* would do for tea, at least so the generality of planters thought; and truly wonderful were the qualities of tea often turned out and despatched to Calcutta to poison the unwary purchaser. "Quantity before quality" was the chief aim; but this maxim, like Boatswain Chuck's "Duty before decency," led in the end to sad and untoward results. The uneven fermenting, sometimes green and sometimes sour; the careless firing, often resulting in burnt tea; the large percentage of coarse leaf plucked, of which nothing but "red leaf" could be made; and the astounding dodges which ingenious planters were up to in order to work up their red leaf into something saleable,—ranging from the simple processes of packing it just as it was, or pulverizing it till it looked like a mixture of red and black pepper, to the more ambitious ideas of making it into "bricks" like Thibetan tea, or damping it in coarse bags and rolling it therein to give it a fictitious colour and curl, and christening it *monmára* and other deceptive names; all these expedients to pull up the outturn resulted eventually in sending down prices to their lowest level, and in causing Assam tea in general to be looked upon as a synonym for senna or slow poison.

By the way, notwithstanding the care now taken with the manufacture of Indian teas, I fear that a discovery of Mr. C. Baber, the British Consul at Chung-Ching, is likely to prove fatal to our Assam tea. Who will purchase it if Mr. Baber's friends, the monks of Mount O-mi, can be induced to send the produce of *their* peculiar tea bushes into the market? Mr. Baber's discovery is so curious that I must quote the extract from his report referring to the matter, drawing attention to the assertion that his unnatural tea bushes grow *wild*. Thus his discovery is not only calculated to ruin the sale of ordinary teas, which are not naturally flavoured with milk and sugar, but to upset my pet theory that no tea grows wild in China. I am afraid some readers will repeat the name of the mountain, "Oh my," in various tones; others may add a syllable and make it O-mi-i.

"In the mountainous region west of Kiating I discovered two kinds of tea of so unexpected a nature that I scarcely venture to mention them. In the monasteries on Mount O-mi, or, as it is locally named, for brevity's sake, Mount O, I was regaled by the monks with an infusion of tea which is naturally sweet, tasting like coarse Congou with a plentiful addition of brown sugar. It is only grown on the slopes of the mountain, and by the monks; two days' journey further west no one had even heard of its existence. I did not see the plant growing, and it is just possible that it is not tea at all. The prepared leaf, however, has all the appearance of tea, and no one on whom I have tried the experiment has taken it for anything else, or remarked upon its peculiarity beyond inquiring why I put so much sugar in it. I am forwarding a specimen to Shanghai, without giving any hint of its singularity, for professional examination, in order that a tea inspector's report may be appended to these notes.

"The other variety, preposterous as the statement may appear, has a natural flavour of milk, or perhaps more exactly, of butter. What is more interesting than this oddity is the fact that it is wild tea growing in its native elevated *habitat* without any aid from human cultivation. An unimpeachable instance of a wild tea plant has never yet been adduced in China. It has been supposed to occur in Formosa, but the specimens I found in the north of that Island had evidently strayed from cultivation. The practice of drinking an infusion made from the wild plant has, I believe, never been met with anywhere. The wild tea in question is found in the uninhabited wilderness west of Kiating and south of Yachou, at heights of 6,000 feet and upwards, and was described to me as a leafy shrub fifteen feet high, with a stem some four inches thick. The wild mulberry is found in the same locality. Every part of the plant, except the root, is used for making the infusion. The wood is chopped up and put into a kettle of water with the dried leaves and twigs, and being boiled yields a strongly coloured but weak tea, possessing a buttery flavour, which gives it a certain resemblance to the Thibetan preparation. It cannot be obtained in Yachou. The only place where I found it in use is the Huang-mu-ch'ang plateau, a terrace perched among the stupendous gorges of the Tung river. I only brought away a small quantity, which unluckily was drunk by mistake; but I hope next summer to take a general botanical expedition to the district, when it will be easy to procure a plentiful specimen." *

I am morally certain that if Mr. Baber had only gone to the spot where these curious tea-bushes grow, and picked up a specimen of the surrounding soil or stones, he would have found they tasted of buttered toast, or muffins.

But to return to our own prosaic cup of tea. The great advantage of the rolling machines now in use seems to be in the speed with which the work can be got through; I hardly think the best of them can give the finish and "twist" to the leaf that an experienced

* This was written fifteen years ago. We have heard no more of these curious tea.

tea-house *sirdar* could do in the hand-rolling days. However, the labour which is saved by the machine is enormous; and where coolies are so often scarce, and gardens so often short of men, as in Assam, the release of a number of able-bodied men from the tea-house, just at the time when they are most required to keep down the fast growing jungle, is a great boon. There are several machines in use: Jackson's, Kinmond's, Nelson's, Lyle's, and others; and planters have their particular fancies about them of course. The one which I saw most in use in my short tour, was either Kinmond's or Jackson's, or a mixture of both. From what I heard I concluded that one of these gentlemen had adopted some little peculiarity of the other in his machine and so infringed his patent; result, a law-suit, of course, and a heavy royalty on all the mixed machines. I did not attend closely to the account given to me of the affair, I am afraid, and the result is that I am about as much mixed in the matter as the machine itself is. However, the Jackson-Kinmond, or Kinmond-Jackson machine, whichever it may be, seemed to be the favourite.

Great care is now bestowed on the fermenting and firing, the only two processes remaining for the rolled leaf to go through. Of course, as in everything else, differences of opinion exist: some fire off almost immediately after rolling; some ferment slightly; some, very much. Nothing but a thorough knowledge of the particular colour and flavor just then in favour in the market, and the exact amount of fermenting and firing necessary to produce that, will serve here. This knowledge can only be gained by watching the tea reports, and by experience. The great thing would seem to be to get the tea *evenly* fermented, and not to squeeze or flatten out the rolled leaf too much in the process: almost every one has his own peculiar way of attaining these *desiderata*. The firing also requires great care and watchfulness, to hit off the happy medium between letting the tea get sour over too slow a fire, smoking it with bad or imperfectly burnt charcoal, and burning it by too brisk a heat. An arrangement now used in supersession of the old-fashioned *dhols* struck me as being a very good one. A masonry compartment, into which several square wire sieves are fitted like drawers, over the one fire, seems both economical and efficient: the upper and lower sieves can be interchanged as the tea in each needs more or less heat. The great want seems to be a good drying machine: several are in existence I believe, but I was not fortunate enough to see one.* Passing a blast of hot air through the tea seems to be the object to be attained; probably some of the lately invented machines may have attained this object with good practical effect. In theory it is simple enough, as many things are which are difficult to work out practically.

The sifting of the different qualities, and the packing of the tea for despatch, though important in their way, are matters of less moment. Tea of a good quality cannot be much spoiled in sifting; it can of course be bro-

---

* Since this was written, I have seen many drying and also sifting machines. Of these, I think the consensus of opinion seems in favour of Davidson's "Sirocco" dryer, and Ansell's Sifter.

ken considerably by pressing too roughly through the sieves, but the flavour and aroma given by careful fermenting and firing are present even in the dust and broken tea. The sieves used are generally wire, the meshes varying from four to the inch (*i.e.*, sixteen to the square inch), to ten or even twelve, I believe; but there is much variety in the number used for the same class of tea, some using a finer sieve for their Pekoe, or whatever they term their finest class of tea, than others. Sieves of cane are sometimes used, and are preferred by some planters, as breaking the tea less, and preserving the "bloom" of it better.

Before packing, a final firing is always given, as tea soon absorbs moisture, especially in the moist climate of Assam, and it is necessary to have it thoroughly dried, and even hot, when packed, otherwise it would probably turn out perfectly musty on reaching its destination, notwithstanding all care in the main processes of manufacture. The chief classes of tea generally made, and the number of sieve used (*number* of sieve meaning number of meshes to the linear inch) are, Congou, left in No. 4; Souchong, in No. 6; Pekoe Souchong, in No. 8; and Pekoe, in No. 10. Orange Pekoe is, I think, merely ordinary Pekoe with a larger number of "nibs," the produce of the "tip," or unopened leaf-bud at the top of the shoot on the bush, in it. Broken tea of the above-named classes, broken mixed, dust, and fannings, with a sprinkling of stalks and general rubbish, bring up the rear, and cover the whole outturn of the garden; the broken mixed, dust, and fannings containing the "wastage" of the sieves, the red leaf (hand picked out of the tea before sifting), and other miscellaneous items, such as odds and ends of bamboo, cane, and dirt, sometimes. To the credit of the planter I must confess I never found any box nails in any class of tea, however humble.

Having so far enlightened the suffering public on the mysteries of tea manufacture, I will wind up with sundry utterly disjointed and spasmodic remarks on labour, emigration, means of communication, enticing each others' coolies away, and various other subjects about which I know little or nothing; for which reason I am confident that my remarks will prove highly interesting.

The having arrived, so to speak, at the dregs of my cup of tea, has suggested a mournful train of thought. Everything in this transitory life must come to an end, even a pleasure trip to Assam; and I can only console myself as Artemus Ward consoled his daughter when she plaintively enquired, "Why do summer roses fade?" Artemus philosophically replied, "Because its their biz; let 'em fade." Even so; cups of tea are made to be drunk, if not spilled or otherwise wasted meanwhile, so it is no use moralizing over the dregs. But in tune with the melancholy emotions which are palpitating beneath my manly waistcoat at recalling the thoughts of bidding adieu to the old familiar friends and scenes amidst which the innocent days of my verdant youth were spent, let me have a dismal croak over tea in general, and its prospects. Some time ago the London correspondent of the *Indian Tea Gazette*, while apparently suffering from dyspepsia, waxed very mournful over the prospects of tea planters. Starting with the cheerful assertion that from first to last more money has been lost than made in tea; that tea is being cultivated now in other countries besides India and China (America for one, I believe); and that prices have been abnormally low, and persisted in remaining so for ever so long, while trade is greatly depressed in England, the chief market for Indian teas; he arrives at the inspiriting conclusion that supply is on the verge of exceeding demand, that extensions are a fraud, and new gardens a delusion and a snare. No doubt a good deal of the foregoing is, to a certain extent, true; but, on the other hand, it must be remembered that many of the causes which produced the depression in trade in general and in tea prices in particular, are merely temporary; already general trade has shown marked signs of improvement; freights lately climbed up to a giddy height, much to some people's disgust—but one man's meat is proverbially another man's poison; and the price of tea took a sudden jump in the home market which must have put a good pile into the pocket of some lucky shippers, though it could not have done much good to producers in general. Again, Indian tea is not largely consumed in many countries as yet, and its use is capable of immense extension; while any concern which has capital at its back, and can afford to place its own teas direct in the home market, waiting awhile for the return; or is able to live over an unfavourable season and bad prices without being cramped for money to carry on the following season;

is bound to do well in the end, notwithstanding the long faces and dismal growls one sees and hears occasionally. Bad seasons and low prices are dangerous only to such gardens or concerns as are worked on the hand-to-mouth principle, and are obliged to hypothecate the coming crop for funds to produce it. Tea in itself is a great fact which may fluctuate, but cannot fail. Wherever middlemen of any kind come in between producer and consumer, they must make a profit, otherwise they would have no *raison d'être*; and this profit is, of course, out of the producer's pocket. Moreover, advances are made by the middlemen for which interest has to be paid; all stock, implements, and stores are purchased by them—and they must, in fairness, have a commission for their trouble; and so on *ad infinitum*. I think it must be self-evident that tea planters who work chiefly through Calcutta agents, or are in their hands to any extent, are heavily handicapped. A bad season or two, a long spell of low prices, or any other cause which may reduce the value of the produce of the garden, throws the planter almost entirely into the agent's hands; and eventually he is swallowed up, and goes the way of so many others, while his garden is abandoned, or flourishes in the hands of its new owners, the men of capital. The moral of all which is, *not* that Calcutta agents are tea-garden devouring monsters, crunching the bones of confiding planters, and assimilating hundreds of acres of smiling cultivation which are the result of the labour and outlay of others; but merely that people with small capital should find some other method of fooling it away than "going into tea" single-handed. It is merely another example of the inexorable law of nature, the survival of the fittest.

I am firmly of opinion that to Calcutta Agency firms is due a great portion of the permanent success which the tea interest has attained. They have often propped up tottering concerns, or tided stranded proprietors over shallows, and otherwise been the backbone of many a shaky garden—of course for a consideration; and it is but natural, and for the good of tea in general, (though the individual go to the wall) that when it is evident the tottering, stranded, or shaky proprietor can no longer be kept going, the *deus ex machinâ* should step forward and reap the benefit of its previous efforts to keep the concern floating. For which candid opinion I quite expect to be scalped by the first small private planter whom I may meet out on the war-path during my next visit to Assam. *Dulce et decorum est pro patriâ mori*; and I shall render up my curly wig (I was bald long ago, and have only a wig and my eyebrows to be "scalped" off) with the peaceful consciousness that I have done my duty by my adopted country, Assam, in warning off men who have just money enough to open out a garden, or buy one ready-made, but not enough to work it without borrowing on the current season's crop, or to tide over a bad season; they are bound to go to the wall. But this is no argument against tea as a good sound investment for capital; far from it. Like the brook

"Men may come, and men may go,
But *tea* goes on for ever!"

One of the great rocks ahead of the Assam tea planter is the cooly. He costs a great deal to procure; he has been legislated about, and brought under the operation of Acts, and the care of cooly-protectors, till his unfortunate employer hardly knows whether he is worth having or not under the circumstances. Steamer captains are worried out of their wits about him, with the multifarious papers they have to sign connected with him, the water tanks they must provide for him, and the proper scale of diet to keep him between the Scylla of starvation and Charybdis of overfeeding while on his way up the river. Doctors and magistrates have to inspect him and pass him, before he is shipped, at sundry places *en route*, and when he is landed; and the only person who can, in my conception, look on the cooly with unmixed complacency, as "a thing of beauty and a joy for ever," is the coolie doctor on the steamer, who gets so much per head for landing him right side uppermost. Arrived on the garden, he has to be housed comfortably; and—as he generally insists on getting seriously ill immediately on arrival—kept in hospital, carefully tended, and supplied with "medical comforts" (including port wine and sago), such as the Rajah of his country never dreamt of. If he is sufficiently amenable to reason not to die, he is valuable to the planter for about two out of his three years' agreement period. After he is "seasoned" he does his work well, and gets on to his own and his employer's satisfaction. After this period, however, he again becomes an object for tender solicitude and care; he is "time-expired" and must be treated with the deference due to his exalted position. Bonuses must be administered to him; his pay raised; extra blankets or some other allurement offered; and unlimited opportunities afforded him of doing "double *hazris*"; all to tempt him to remain on the garden now that he has really commenced to be worth the money and care expended on him. Meanwhile the neighbouring planters are all doing their best to entice him away by better offers—he is a free agent now, remember—and so he learns his value in the market, is taught to hold his head high, and be "cheeky"; secure in the knowledge of past prosecutions for assault and grievous hurt, that his long suffering master must be sorely aggravated before attempting to "Fullerize" him as he deserves.

Planters' Associations have been got up, no doubt, and in some districts are flourishing as they deserve to do; but in some places the introduction of a rule binding members not to entice each other's coolies away has been the signal for the withdrawal of more or less members, and perhaps the breaking up of the Association. Once half a dozen planters in a district repudiate an attempt to introduce the non-enticement rule, it is useless for any to hold to it; they only tie their hands and place themselves at a disadvantage as compared with their less scrupulous neighbours. Various are the dodges of enticing; higher bonuses; higher rates of pay; promising to employ them only on such work as they can earn "doubles" at (*i.e.*, working on a task); and also importing batches of young women, whose attractions often prove irresistible in seducing the gay and well-to-do time-expired Bengali Don Juans from neighbouring gardens.

Chota Nagpur appears to be the best recruiting field, Opinions are divided as to the class of labourers best suited for Assam. In out-of-the-way places the "jungly", as the Chota Nagpur coolie is called, appears to do best. Coolies from the North-West and Madras are less handy at improvising and at obtaining comforts for themselves under difficulties, and require to be close to large bazars. The coolies from the North-West, having more caste prejudices, and knowing better how to assert themselves, give more trouble than the Madras coolie. As to local labour, practically it is nothing; in exceptional gardens, favourably situated, Mikirs, Assamese, and occasionally even Nagas, can be induced to work, but only spasmodically as a rule, and they cannot be depended on. The Kacharis are more reliable, but are not very numerous. The Assamese as a rule will not work, except perhaps on clearing a new garden, or after several bad harvests, when the local stocks of food grains are very low; but as long he can grow, or procure readily, enough rice to keep body and soul together, with a trifle of opium now and then, he will not work.

THE OPENING OF THE ASSAM RAILWAY.

THE COMPANY AND THE LINE.

VERY few years ago, Assam was only known to our friends at home as a shadowy vague sort of place, somewhere beyond the confines of civilization, whither "ne'er do weel" younger brothers or other male relatives, who could not pass for the services, or get a respectable situation anywhere else, might be sent to be converted into "planters". Assam was accredited with producing and exporting a very strong variety of tea, somewhat unpleasant to the unaccustomed palate; a peculiar and aggravated species of fever; an unusual number of invalids suffering from liver and spleen; and a high percentage of corpses. The latter, however, were not exported as a rule. Assam was also understood to import and consume a quantity of spirituous liquors and tobacco altogether disproportionate to its size and population. And there the knowledge of Assam acquired by the average Britisher ended.

The extraordinary fertility of the soil of Assam; its capabilities as a great rice producing country, in the hands of cultivators a little more energetic than the lazy opium-eating Assamese; its almost unknown and unexplored mineral treasures—coal, iron, gold and other metals; its magnificient forests—in short its almost unrivalled resources which only awaited development; all these things were unknown to the world in general outside of Assam; and indeed they were thought little of by those in Assam, except the few who could see beyond the limits of their tea gardens, and discern the great future open to the province, if its other resources could be developed as rapidly as its tea had been.

But it is a difficult place to get anything done in. The native Assamese is a helpless sort of animal, from whom little or no assistance towards developing the resources of the country can be expected. The labour question is the dismal swamp in which every project for developing Assam has hitherto been stifled, and yet the Assamese can and has worked, and produced magnificent buildings and splendid roads. The ruins of the former are found all over the country; and the old *rajalli*, which we occasionally stumble across in the forest still, in its decay, laughs to scorn the unpy efforts of our Public Works Department on our modern roads. But in those days there was no enlightened Government to prohibit forced labour; and the P.W.D. contractor and sub-contractor had not then been invented.

In a sketch of the rise and progress of the Assam Railway and Trading Company, the peculiar difficulties of the country, and the necessity of importing every kind of labour, not only skilled mechanics and artificers, but even the common cooly, must be borne in mind. The further facts of the railway being begun at the far end of what is now a recognized scheme of through communication, and that stock and material of all kinds had, in addition to the usual import charges, a long and expensive inland river journey to pay for, must also be taken into consideration to enable a fair estimate to be made of the difficulties under which the Assam Railway and Trading Company brought the first portion of its undertakings to a successful issue.

It is practically to the unremitting energy and perseverance of one man, Dr. J. Berry-White, Brigade Surgeon, Bengal Army, retired, that the Company owes its existence and success, and Assam generally is indebted for the first great stride towards the development of its mineral wealth. The idea of an Assam Railway Company originated in a somewhat fortuitons manner. During the rainy season of 1878, Mr. Berry-White (then, as for many previous years, chief Military and Civil Surgeon to Government in Upper Assam), while on leave at Shillong, received several letters from friends of his, tea planters on the Sadya Road, representing the almost impassable state of that road. Owing to the recent immense increase of traffic on the road, and the want of timely repairs, the planters pointed out that their communications threatened soon to be entirely cut off; and unless something were done, they apprehended that they would shortly be unable to ship their produce, or get up food for their coolies.

These representations were of such an urgent character that Mr. White laid them before the Chief Commissioner, then Sir Steuart Bayley, and Colonel Trevor his Chief Engineer, for consideration. Mr. White suggested that, as it was impossible to keep unmetalled roads in order with the annually increasing traffic, and as the most imperfect form of metalling, that is with broken brick, cost about Rs. 1,000 per mile, it would be almost as cheap, and much more advantageous, to have a permanent iron way of some sort; either a tramway, or a light railway. After several interviews and discussions on the subject, Sir Steuart Bayley agreed to recommend the Government of India to sanction an annual subsidy of Rs. 80,000 for a line of light railway from the steamer ghat at Dibrugarh to Saikwa on the Brahmaputra opposite Sadya.

A further examination into details showed, however, that the probable traffic would not pay the working expenses, even when supplemented by the subsidy; and the scheme threatened to fall through. At this stage, however, Mr. White suggested a branch line from Dumduma to Makum, to open up the great mineral wealth—coal, petroleum, etc., known to exist in that neighbourhood; and pointed out that thus an abundant and remunerative traffic would be secured for the proposed railway. On this the Chief Commissioner promised that he would recommend an extra subvention of Rs. 20,000 per annum for the Makum or coal-field branch, making a total of a lakh of rupees annually; if, on the other hand, Mr. White and his friends could raise the necessary capital to construct the line, and to thoroughly exploit the mineral and timber resources of Makum. Mr. White then placed himself in communication with Messrs. Shaw, Finlayson &. Co., then the Agents to his tea estates in Dibrugarh. The firm at once agreed to finance the several undertakings on the proposed terms. A correspondence ensued between the Governments of India and Assam which occupied nearly a year, and resulted in the grant to Messrs. Shaw, Finlayson Co. of three several concessions.—

(1) To construct a railway in the Dibrugarh district, with conditional subvention of Rs. 1,00,000.

(2) The working of the entire Makum Coal-fields, then in the hands of Government.

(3) The exclusive right to fell timber, for half a mile on each side of the Makum branch line, on payment of the ordinary royalties.

On the 8th December 1879, under the impression that they had secured sufficient support to warrant them in so doing, Messrs. Shaw, Finlayson & Co. brought out on the London market "The Assam Railway Co., Ld." reserving to themselves the coal and timber concessions. The subscription received from the public, however, was not sufficient to warrant the Directors in proceeding to allotment; the Company therefore remained abortive. An engineer with a small staff of European and native assistants had been despatched to Dibrugarh by Messrs. Shaw, Finlayson & Co., but owing to the failure to float the Company on the London market, they had to be dismissed, and the whole scheme remained in abeyance for nearly a year. Indeed, many who had not faith in the solidity of the project, and the energy and perseverance of its originator, believed it had totally collapsed, and looked upon the Assam Railway as one of those chimerical and Utopian schemes which would be very beneficial if they could only be brought within the bounds of practicability. The Sadya Road planters resigned themselves to their accustomed rainy season miseries—the impassable roads, broken carts, damaged teas, and hungry coolies, mutinous at long delayed rice supplies.

The period of collapse did not last long. Before the year was over, the scheme was brought under the notice of Mr. Benjamin Piercy, M.I.C.E., of Marchwick Hall, Denbighshire, and No. 8, Drapers Gardens, London. This gentleman had constructed and successfully financed the entire railway system of Sardinia, several lines in Wales, and various railways in other parts of the world. Mr. Piercy agreed to take up the project, provided that all the concessions were thrown into one great company. This was to include the petroleum concession, then in the hands of a private company, in which Mr. Berry-White was the chief shareholder. He also stipulated that the statements put before him as to the mineral wealth to be developed by the scheme, and the capabilities of the project generally, should be verified by his own trusted agents. This having been arranged, Mr. Benjamin Piercy deputed his brother, Mr. Robert Piercy, to report on the prospects of the various enterprises. In the early part of 1881, Mr. Robert Piercy accordingly proceeded to Assam, and, during a stay of several weeks in the neighbourhood, thoroughly investigated the mineral wealth of Makum. He reported that "the coal-fields of Makum were vastly greater in quantity and better in quality, than had ever before been suspected," "that a railway such as proposed could be constructed for under Rs. 4,000 per mile," and that "the whole scheme promised to turn out a most remunerative investment." On this report a syndicate was formed, composed for the most part of Mr. B. Piercy's personal or business friends, which decided to go into the project; and on the 30th July 1881, the "Assam Railway and Trading Company, Limited" was incorporated with a capital of £350,000 in preferred shares of £10 each, and £43,750 in deferred shares of £1 each.

On the 2nd August 1881 the prospectus was advertised in the leading London newspapers; and by noon of the same day the Company's bankers had received applications for shares to an amount of twenty-eight per cent. in excess of the capital sought for. Since then a further sum of £250,000 has been raised by the issue of debentures—the aggregate share and debenture capital being now over £600,000.

Some time was taken up in the survey of the line from the ghat to the town, and in getting possession of the required lands; and the works were not fairly commenced until 1st January 1882, when the best portion of that working season may be said to have passed. The difficulties and drawbacks were at first heartbreaking and apparently insurmountable. Allusion has before been made to the peculiar nature of these difficulties in Assam, and it would be tedious to detail how obstacle after obstacle arose and was surmounted. Bearing in mind the, so to speak, isolated situation of the work, far from any manufacturing centre, even of the smallest kind, and from any sort of labour market; and noting the generally incredulous and sometimes half hostile attitude taken locally, it will be readily admitted that, although no very great engineering difficulties, such as the great bridges of other Indian railways, had to be encountered, still the enterprise laboured under disadvantages peculiarly its own. Planters looked askance at works which were offering more than double the prevailing rates of the district for labour, and bemoaned the certain desertion of all their time-expired coolies, and the secession of their scanty local labour force. Officals and station residents bewailed the rise in the price of provisions, in the wages of domestic servants, in house rent, and in everything generally. "The railway would ruin the district," was the burden of the cry heard all round. But, as a matter of fact, the high wages offered attracted practically no garden labour. A few coolies here and there left the tea gardens to "pick up rupees," as they fondly imagined, on the railway; but the contrast of camping out and doing task work in all weathers was great, when compared with their comfortable lines, little vegetable gardens, small tasks at which they could easily earn "doubles," and general comfort, on the tea estates. That the influx of numerous Europeans should raise prices of food and domestic service was only to be expected, but the labour market was very little, if at all, disturbed. The railway company imported its own labour, as well as its European staff; it built and purchased bungalows for its superior officers; comfortably hutted in its mechanics, etc.; and generally interfered with local arrangements as little as could possibly be expected in a so out of the way a place, where demand could not be naturally and promptly met by supply. The number of Europeans employed on the works and at the mines during the progress of construction was about one hundred. Of these sixty-nine were brought out direct from Europe. The number of artisans and coolies imported from other districts from the commencement to the opening of the line was 5,872; and the amount of money spent locally averaged nearly a lakh of rupees per mensem, the total local expenditure for the whole period having been about Rs. 21,80,000. Dating from the commencement of the works in January 1882, the progress made can best be shown chronologically as follows. On the 1st May 1882, the first locomotive engine in Assam passed over the section of the line from the steamer ghat to the Jaipur Road. On the 15th August, the section to the Dinjan River, fifteen miles, was opened for goods traffic, and on 23rd December, 20 miles of line, to Chabwa, was open for goods traffic. On the 16th July 1883, about eighteen months after the commencement of the works, the line to the Makum junction, 40 miles in length, including the double ghat line (to the upper and lower steamer ghats), was opened for passenger traffic under sanction from the Government of India. Meanwhile the line was being laid from the other end at Makum, engines and materials having been boated up the Dehing River; and on Christmas Day 1883, the rails were joined near Borbhil, completing railway communication from the banks of the Dehing at Makum, or Margherita, as it is now called, to the Brahmaputra. A Christmas distribution of Makum coal to the residents of the station marked the auspicious occasion. The railway company forgot to add the usual soup and blankets to their Christmas distribution.

The objects aimed at by the Company have been already partially specified. The railway was originally projected to facilitate the traffic along the Sadya Road, which traffic, owing to the opening out of numerous large tea gardens along the length of the road, from Dibrugarh to near the Saikwa Ghat, had become far too heavy for the existing *kutcha* road. It having been found, however, that with the carriage of rice and other stores up, and of tea down, the projected line would not pay working expenses, the branch to Makum to open out the coal-fields, was added to the original scheme; and the continuation of the main line to Saikwa Ghat, at first stipulated for as a military necessity, was given up. The main line terminus was fixed at Talup, a large tea estate belonging to R. Gordon Shaw, Esq., and the furthest large garden on the road. The endeavour to float a railway company, as a carrying company pure and simple, having failed, the present company was incorporated both as a carrying and trading company; having the several concessions regarding coal, petroleum and timber, already specified; mining rights and general powers to trade in the various mineral and other products granted to it by the concessions.

The terminus on the Brahmaputra is at a point some four miles below the town of Dibrugarh, known as Mohana Mukh, which is the steamer ghat during the dry season. From there the line passes over low ground and rice fields for about a mile and a half;

then rises on an embankment for about a mile further, till it reaches the branch for the Dibru Mukh, the steamer ghat during the rainy season. In the space between the two branches, or just below the junction of the upper and lower ghat line, are situated the stores, the workshops, the locomotive and carriage sheds, and the houses of a number of the European mechanics and workmen. Further down the upper, or rainy season ghat line, and close to where the Dibru River debouches into the Brahmaputra, are several bungalows for the upper employés of the Company.

Below these bungalows, the dry bed of the river was utilized as a natural but efficient dockyard for the Company's Flotilla; and here several flats for the conveyance of the coal, timber, and other products down the river were built. Returning to the junction or bifurcation of the two ghat lines, the railway proceeds thence in an easterly direction over an existing road known as the Amlah patti, the houses on each side of this road being generally occupied by the Amlah or native court officials. Crossing the Sibsagar Road—the Grand Trunk Road of Assam—the line approaches Dibrugarh, and reaches the Rehabari Station, 3¼ miles from the steamer ghat.

The town of Dibrugarh, the capital of the Lakhimpur district, and the chief military station in the Assam Valley, was first selected as a site for a station in the years 1838 to 1840, by General Hamilton Vetch, then Captain Vetch, Political Agent in Upper Assam. The principal buildings are the Kacherri, the Jail, the

Fort, the Church, and the "Planters Stores," while there are numerous bungalows occupied by the officials of the district, planters, and other gentlemen whose business makes a residence in the station necessary The Church was built by the late General Reid, R.A., from a design by Pugin, out of a fund collected as a memorial to the late Colonel White, who was killed at Sadya in a night attack on that post by the Kamptis. His remains are interred under the tower of the building. The population of the town is estimated at about 10,000, of whom over 100 are Europeans. It is believed that the population given in the last census has more than doubled since the commencement of the railway.

From the Rehabari Station the railway line runs through a tea garden of the British India Co., then crosses the Mankatta Road, leaving on the right hand the new workshop of the Public Works Department, and the Chokidingi tea estate. After a mile and a half through ryots' cultivation and skirting a suburban road, it enters on the Jaipur Road, with a rather sharp curve, at a place now known as Rai Bahadur's, the ancestral homestead of the Naga Hazarus. This Naga Hazaru was an hereditary post held by a Mattak family under the Assam Rajah, their functions being to conduct negotiations between the Nagas and other hill tribes, and the Assam Durbar. These duties are still continued for the British Government by the present representatives of the family, Lahmon Dass and Haddan Dass, on both of whom the title of Rai Bahadur and the honorary rank of extra Assistant Commissioner have been conferred as a recognition of their long and faithful services. Directly opposite to the Rai Bahadur's is a road leading into the military cantonments, and a little further along the line, on the left, is the tea estate of the late Colonel Hanney, now the property of General Holroyd. Beyond, or, indeed, partially in this tea garden, is the race-course; the new iron roof of the grand stand being visible from the railway line. From here to Lahoal, the next station, the railway is laid on the Jaipur Road. About a mile from the Chaulkwa garden, the rum distillery and tea garden belonging to Mr. A. Scott Campbell, brother of the energetic Deputy Commissioner of Kamrup, is reached. Passing for some two miles more through tea and rice cultivation, the Bokel factory and bungalow, belonging to the Jokai (Assam) Tea Co., are seen on the right. A siding connects the railway with the Bokel tea-house. A little further on a road branches off to the left, leading to the Attabari tea garden of the same company, upon which estate a colony of upwards of 300 native Christians, chiefly Kols from Chota Nagpur, is settled. A mile further the Lahoal factory and garden are passed. This property belonged to the Mattack Tea Co., now amalgamated with the Jokai (Assam) Co. A very short distance beyond this, the train stops at the Lahoal Station, 10¼ miles from the steamer ghat, and 6½ miles from Rehabari. Close to the station, on the right, is the Kalijan garden of the Wilton Tea Co. At this point the railway leaves the Jaipur Road, and follows the Sadya Road to its terminus on the main line. About a mile and a quarter beyond Lahoal the Sherwood tea estate is passed on the left. This, formerly the property of Mr. R. F. Cavendish, has recently been purchased by the Jokai Co.

For some four miles further the line passes through rice cultivation, which is, however, hidden from view by a narrow belt of forest lining the road. At the 15th mile the Dinjan is crossed. This is the first bridge of any magnitude on the line—it is 56 feet in span, in four openings—and, like all other bridges on the main line, is constructed entirely of timber; the posts being Nabor (*Mesua Ferrea*), the indigenous ironwood of Assam, and the beams of Ajhar, (*Lagerstrœmia Reginæ*), believed to be the best timber tree of the country. It may be noted here, once for all, that there are numerous culverts on the main line and branches, some of masonry and others of tubes of corrugated iron, patented by the District Engineer, Mr. Aloys Sprenger. On crossing the Dinjan, the line passes between two large tea estates; that on the left being the property of the Nahortolli Tea Co. and on the right the Dikam garden, the local head-quarters of the Wilton Tea Co. About two miles further the Nadua Road junction is passed on the left; this road being the outlet for several tea gardens situated on or near it. For some three miles further the line is bordered by grass and forest land; till between the 19th and 20th miles, the Ridgeway garden on the left, and the Sialkoti garden on the right, are passed; the latter being the property of Mr. Walter S. Warren. The Hiloidari garden of the Chabwa Tea Company adjoins the Sialkoti garden; and at the 20th mile the Chabwa Station is reached, 16 miles from Rehabari.

Chabwa, or Cha-bowa, as its name implies, is a place where tea was sown; and here, it may be noted, was the first tea garden ever planted in India. It was originally established by Government as an experiment as to whether tea could be cultivated in this country as a remunerative industry, and consequently it may be regarded as the birthplace of the great Indian tea enterprise. Government having satisfied itself that tea could be grown successfully, retired, and made over the garden to a Chinaman named Among. From want of capital he failed, and the garden was purchased for a few hundred rupees by the late James Warren, whose nephews are among the largest tea proprietors in the district.

From Chabwa the railway passes for three or four miles through forest and grass land, with occasional clearings made by time expired coolies from tea gardens, who are settling down in considerable numbers along the line, till at the 26th mile the first portion of the Panitolla tea estates is reached. These gardens, the property of Mr. J. Berry-White, extend along both sides of the road to the 29th mile, the Panitolla station being situated at the 27th mile.

From this station a road on the left leads to Rangagora, formerly a military post, and now the centre of an extensive group of tea gardens. Between Panitolla and Tinsukia, the line runs through heavy forest and grass. At Tinsukia a road to the right, the old "Tengrai Alli," leads to a group of tea concerns on the east bank of the Tengrai River; another road to the left leads to some tea gardens on the Rangagora Road. Tinsukia was, in former days, the residence of the Mattack Gohains or high priests. Large tanks and the ruins of masonry buildings indicate the former dwellings of these chiefs. Many of their descendants still live in the locality, but have gradually merged into the condition of ordinary ryots. At the 35th mile the Hukanpukhri tea estate, the property of Mr. J. B. White, commences, and extends on the left side of the road to the 37th mile. Opposite to it, between the 36th and 37th miles, is the Loharijan garden, belonging to Mr. S. B. Goad. At 38¾ miles from the steamer ghat the Makum junction is reached.

The Makum branch, 23 miles in length from the junction to Margherita on the Dehing, runs almost entirely through heavy forest composed chiefly of magnificent trees, the growth of centuries. The] principal varieties of timber met with are Nahor, *(Mesua ferrea)*; Sam, *(Artocarpus chaplasha)*; Gunserai *(Cinnamomem glanduliferum)*, and, indeed, nearly every variety of timber tree indigenous to Assam. After leaving the junction, cultivation, either of tea or rice, is no longer seen; and every vestige of human habitation disappears. Four bridges are crossed on this branch—the Tingrai, 34 feet long, in two spans of ten feet each and one of fourteen; the Borbhil, of two spans, each 22 feet; the Digboi, three spans, each 20 feet; and the Powai, two spans of 25 feet each. The Bor Dehing bridge is 800 feet long, in spans of 50 feet each. It was not quite finished at the formal opening of the line, as the trusses were not in position; but coal trains without a locomotive could be pushed across by hand.

The only station on the Makum branch is at Borbhil, which, from the magnificent forests in its neighbourhood, is likely to become an important timber depôt. After crossing the Dehing bridge, the settlement of Margherita, so called in honour of the Queen of Italy, is reached. This place, sprung up only within the last few months, promises to become an important trade centre; the Nagas, Kamptis, and Singphos resorting to it to sell India-rubber, wax, ebony and other products, and to purchase Manchester, Birmingham and other goods. Several of the large Marwari merchants of Dibrughur have opened branch stores at Margherita; and over 300 tons of goods of various sorts already change hands monthly.

Near the bridge are the workshops and saw mills and the bungalow of the Chief Engineer of this section of the railways.

A path going eastwards through the jungle leads to the petroleum wells, which are reported by experts to be among the richest reservoirs of mineral oil known. The company has been prevented hitherto, by the pressure of other work, from developing this branch of their mineral wealth; but as soon as the railway is completed and the collieries in full swing of working, it is intended to open out the petroleum industry with vigour.

The colliery line from Margherita to Ledo is 6¾ miles, with a short branch to meet the Thikak inclined plane. The line here runs chiefly through old Naga *jhums* or clearings, on which scrub jungle and small trees have grown. The Namdang river is crossed by a bridge of three spans of 50 feet each, and the line ends in the Ledo colliery.

The most interesting feature of this colliery is a number of isolated little hills of coal standing above the surface of the ground. The surface soil has been scraped off one of these curious coal hills, and the quantity of coal estimated is at 50,000 tons, which can be quarried direct into the waggons. From here a path has been cut through the jungle to the Thikak Colliery, ascending some 1,300 feet above Ledo. Here a great coal seam of from 40 to 50 feet thickness has been tunnelled through, the drifts and galleries being nearly a mile in length. The vast quantity of coal which has lain hidden in this hill for ages will be faintly comprehended when it is known that, according to the computations of the mining engineers, *one hundred millions* of tons are estimated to exist above the galleries; and below them, but above the drainage level, *four hundred millions* of tons. Such figures are simply astounding. The coal, moreover, is said to be the best ever found in Asia—the analysis giving the quantity of fixed carbon at 66 per cent., the ash ranging from 1 to 3 per cent. only. Practical tests in locomotives and steamers have proved that the coal, as steam coal, is quite equal to West Hartley or South Wales coal. From the head of the working down to the branch of the colliery line, an inclined plane about a mile in length is in course of construction. This is being laid with a double line of light rails, 2 feet gauge, and will be worked on the automatic principle in use in the collieries in South Wales and elsewhere, the loaded waggons, descending, drawing up the empty waggons by means of a wire rope connecting them, and working over a revolving drum at the top of the incline.

Near this spot some very fine sandstone is being quarried, which makes excellent grindstones, equal to the best imported from Europe.

The coke prepared from both the Ledo and Thikak Collieries is reported to be the best ever made in India, and it is hoped it will eventually entirely supersede the use of charcoal in the manufacture of tea.

Fire clay is found between the seams of coal. This is of excellent quality, and in quantity sufficient to meet the demands of all India.

The Opening Day.

The morning of the 18th February—a day, as Mr. J. Berry White observed at Margherita, to be marked as a red letter day in the Assam Calendar—was as dull, gloomy and dispiriting as its predecessors for some days had been. Driving through the mud in the drizzling rain to the Rehabari Station, it required all our faith in the future of Assam and enthusiasm about the opening of the pioneer mineral enterprise, to prevent some of us from turning back. However, the road, axle deep in mud between the jail road and the Mankatta road, sharpened the contrast between the old and new methods of progress—Public Works road *versus* Assam Railway Company's iron way. The special train was timed to leave Rahabari Station at 7 A.M., but as nearly 200 Europeans had to be collected together, not to mention over 100 of the leading natives—court officials, Marwaris, and various notabilities—and as punctuality is not by any means a Dibrugarh virtue on any occasion, it was wonderful that we actually got off by 7-20 A.M. We stopped again at Rai Bahadur to take up the band of the 42nd Assam Light Infantry (kindly lent for the day by the Colonel) and some more passengers—the officers of the regiment, etc.—and then ran on to the Lahoal Station, which was reached at 7-50. Here a halt, nominally of only a few minutes, was made for coffee, tea and other refreshments (the latter italicised, in the notice sent round, for the benefit of those who despise coffee and tea). But it is hard to get an excursion crowd into a train again, whether on a festive trip to Brighton and back again, or on the way to Makum. There was rather a scramble for coffee, buns and sandwiches ; and whisky was enquired for occasionally, just to keep the damp out of one's throat, you know. The tea and coffee were brewed in a somewhat novel manner; kerosine oil tins (N.B., well cleaned) with brass taps were the tea and coffee pots.

Eight more passengers, all volunteers in uniform and under arms, joined the train here. And here let me note the rapid way the volunteers had been mobilised —to use a big word for a small occasion. Only the day before, the idea was originated to have a volunteer parade and march past before the Chief Commissioner at Margherita as part of the programme of the day. Most of the officers, several non-commissioned officers and a few privates were in Dibrugarh ; but as tea gardens cannot be left entirely to themselves or the native establishment nowadays, the bulk of the Lakhimpur Corps was on its gardens, minding its own peaceful business. Telegrams were sent flying round the district all along the railway line and forwarded by special messengers from the nearest stations to the individuals of the Corps not present in the station. The result, as a proof of the usefulness of the Corps in case of emergency, was really gratifying. A compact little body of European volunteers, enough to prove formidable against any sudden raid of the hill tribes, was collected at Margherita, close under the Naga Hills, within 18 hours notice. The fact speaks for itself and requires no comment.

Leaving Lahoal at 8-10 A.M., the train reached the Makum junction at 10-12, only a little more than half an hour late, having stopped at every station and crossing to pick up altogether some 50 more passengers —volunteers, peaceful planters, and a fair sprinkling of ladies. The line so far is laid on the Sadya road and has already been described. At Tinsukia a telegram was received by Mr J. Berry White, which deserves to be immortalised, if only as a record of the audacity of the sender thereof. His identity is, of course, a deep secret, otherwise he might be found guilty of high treason or some other dreadful crime, for assuming regal and imperial status and forging Her Majesty's name. The telegram ran as follows :—

"From Queen Victoria, Windsor Castle, London, to Dr. J. B. White:—Our royal congratulations on opening Pioneer Provincial Coal Industry. Book our Royal Household three maunds weekly cash rates. Wish you many happy return tickets of the season from the bottom of our royal heart." Her Majesty's business-like instincts saw the advantage of cash rates, and her liberal order evinced her practical interest in the success of the enterprise. At Makum junction there was a sort of a breakfast, but as the whole station would not hold 40 people without crowding and there were about 250 to be fed, the result was a considerable scramble. Most of us managed to get a drink of some sort, according to taste; and there were sandwiches, biscuits and buns in profusion. The latter, being somewhat heavy, were occasionally converted into missiles by a festive few amongst the crowd, and a regular game of bun-balling (if I may coin a word akin to snow-balling) went on for a while. Leaving the junction at 10-30 A.M., the train plunged into the heart of the primeval forest, and surely never from any other railway carriage windows in the world was such a scene viewed as greeted our eyes. South American lines have penetrated tropical forests before now, and have had "considerable jungle" to tackle. But I question if even any of these lines could show such magnificent timber, with such a matted and tangled undergrowth, dense canebrakes, inextricably confused creepers and parasitical growths, as the virgin forest on the Makum branch exhibits. It is useless to attempt a description. The number of men—imported labourers—who were sent home to their countries by the Railway Company, torn, lacerated by the thorns of the Assam *baint*, or cane, and prostrated by malarial fever and its resultant organic diseases, notwithstanding the medical care they received here, testifies to the enormous difficulties encountered and overcome in opening out this branch. Here and there on the line a few huts, and, perhaps, a damp, dripping disconsolate-looking tent appeared—the temporary homes of a gang of workmen and their superior. The desolate dreary look of these patches of humanity in the gloom of the primeval forest, particularly on such a dark drizzling day, gave us a vivid idea of the life led by the working pioneers of this great enterprise. One could picture the cheerless return "home" of these men after a hard day's work, spent with toil, lacerated with thorns, their life blood half drained by leeches, and often, notwithstanding the exertions of those concerned to keep the commissariat arrangements in working order, with but short commons and poor fare to look forward to.

There were occasional heavy cuttings through the ends of spurs, where the line skirted some low hills, and also heavy embankments in the intervening depressions, which must have considerably added to the difficulties of the work. The various bridges crossed —the Lingrai, Digboy, Borbhil, and Powai—were not quite finished, and looked somewhat risky to the nervous, although they were really perfectly safe. Near the Powai bridge the undergrowth seemed lighter, while the forest trees looked more enormous and gigantic than before. The Dehing bridge—a huge timber structure about 80C feet long—was reached at 12-30 P.M. As the trusses were not in position it was deemed unsafe to run the engine across, so it disappeared up a siding and the carriages were hand-shunted across the bridge, one by one, to the Margherita side of the river. During this proceeding we had a fine view of the reaches of the river, up and down stream, and of the opposite bank, steep and high, crowned by the hill on which the bungalow of the Chief Engineer of this branch is built, with the higher hills giving a magnificent background to the scene. After crossing the river, as we had to wait a little while for the engine belonging to the colliery line, which had gone up to Ledo with the Chief Commissioner and party, the volunteers fell in, about forty strong, and just as the Chief arrived from the collieries, were inspected by Major Beauclerk, Commandant, ordered to pile arms, and assemble again on return from the collieries. We then all took our seats again and started for Ledo. It was considerably past one o'clock before we got fairly under weigh for the Ledo Colliery, so we had to give up all idea of a visit to the larger and more interesting mine at Thikak, the residence of the able and energetic Chief Mining Engineer, Mr. Turner. This mine, to which a short branch line turns off from the Ledo line, is situated on the side of a hill, some 1,300 feet above the general level of the country. The train slowed down opposite the branch to give us a leisurely view of the cleared hill side with the Engineer's bungalow and the huts of the workmen dotted about at the head of the workings. The Thikak mine, with its magnificent bed of coal of enormous depth and thickness, through which main galleries and rectangular drifts have been laid out and excavated by Mr. Turner, is, on the authority of the Chief Commissioner, who spent the afternoon of the 17th in going through the galleries, a sight worth seeing and one that must be seen to be realised. It is computed by Mr. Turner, whose experience and special qualifications are unquestionable, that in this coal bed alone over 500,000,000 tons of coal exist—100,000,000 above the present galleries and drifts, and 400,000,000 below them in the body of the hill, but still above drainage level—so that to excavate and utilise this enormous quantity of first class coal, sufficient for the wants of the next two or three generations, absolutely no pumping, no contact with almost the worst enemy of the miner—water—will be needed. An inclined plane, laid with double lines of rails, is made from the head of the workings to the branch of the main colliery line below. This is worked on the automatic principle—the loaded waggons, descending, pulling up the empty ones by means of a wire rope revolving over a "drum." Thus the coal is simply quarried out of the hill side, loaded into the coal-vans, and slides down hill to the coal-trucks on the branch line below. As in the course of years, higher or lower levels are tapped, it is merely a little more or less of the inclined plane. There was a temporary scare some years ago about the gradual exhaustion of existing coal beds, and the question of fuel for future generations was seriously discussed by sundry quasi-scientists. The Thikak mine could meet that question, to use a cricketing phrase, "off its own bat," to say nothing of Ledo and other coal beds conceded to this Company, but as yet barely prospected.

So future generations can make their appearance in this world without troubling their minds on the question of coal. Makum covers the ground.

The line to Ledo runs through old Naga clearings or *jhums*. The fluctuating style of cultivation practised by many of the semi-barbarous tribes in and around Assam—making a rough clearance with axe and fire, squatting (to use a colonial phrase) on the land, sewing and reaping without any practical cultivation for two or three years, and then moving off to fresh fields and pastures new.—is called *jhum* cultivation. Thus the line through Ledo passes through what is merely low scrub and brushwood, as compared with the virgin forest passed through on the other side of the Dehing, though it would pass for fairly heavy jungle in some parts of India! It is merely the luxuriant growth of a few years on the abandoned Naga clearings. On one part of the line there is a rather heavy gradient for some distance, probably about one in sixty. Altogether, there is a considerable rise from Margherita to Ledo, and the engineering difficulties, pure and simple, apart from the unusual physical obstacles presented by the Assam forest, with its accompanying cane-thorns and leeches, are by no means inconsiderable. The line from Margherita to the mine is most skilfully laid out, skirting a series of small hills, and reflects great credit on Chevalier R. Paganini, the Chief Engineer of this section.

We reached Ledo at 2 P.M. and all detrained to inspect. The first curious feeling was that of tramping along over a roadway metalled, so to speak, with small coal, dry and crunching under the feet, on a wet and generally "sloppy" and slippery day. This suggested a query—Could not the Assam Railway and Trading Company generously supply the local D.P.W. with some of the waste small coal and dust to help the wicked to stand in slippery places on the station and suburban roads? The chief road in Dibrugarh—the local Rotten Row—is know as the "Red Road" from the colour of its broken brick metalling. Why not try some "Black Roads" for a change?

We climbed up a little incline—more small coal—and then before us was one of the curious little hills of coal for which Ledo is remarkable. The hill had been scraped or "faced" down and several drifts run into it in various directions. One was run right through the hill out to the other side, and through this novel tunnel Mr. Turner led the lengthy file of visitors. It was a curious sight. The rain had ceased, and an occasional fitful gleam of sunshine was visible. Ladies, a considerable number of whom were present, in all varieties of costume, from the prudent dark-coloured ulster, to the "reckless of weather" gala dress donned in all its glory; gentlemen in still more varieties of costume, ranging from a regular "masher" get up, through the graduations of ordinary morning dress, riding suits, planter's *kamjhari* or "round the garden in the morning" attire, down to the open shirt, loose, fly away coat, turned up corduroys, and big boots of the British workman; natives of all sorts; the Rai Bahadur, gorgeous in many-coloured silks and embroidery; the silver bedecked and red or yellow turbaned

Kyahs or Marwaris; the sober grey and black *chapkan* of the court amlah; the shawl, transparent muslin *dhoty*, long stockings, and patent leather shoes of the ubiquitous Bengali Babu, down to the next to nudity of the coolies standing round. Picture a file of pilgrims, nearly 500 strong, in all these varieties of costume, personally conducted, not by Cook, but by Mr. Turner, the Mining Engineer, along a tunnel of coal, right through the base of a hill—a Naga hill too—I am afraid to say how long. It was too dark to think of pacing it, or of anything but scrambling out of the blackness of darkness (no lights were taken) into Heaven's blessed daylight on the other side.

More coal, more drifts on all sides, till one seemed involved in a labyrinth of coal, and to be suffering from coal on the brain. A circuitous open-air path brought us to our ingress point again, and thence most of us started uphill for the upper Ledo seam, away up several hundred feet on another hill side. We started, I say; but few reached the goal. Some adventurous spirits not only reached the workings there, but surmounted the crest of the hill above them, whence they waved and screamed derision to the panting and perspiring pilgrims beneath them. Their glory was evanescent, however, as sublunary glories are, even at Makum. The engine's shrill and repeated whistles brought them tearing down the inclined plane from the head of the upper workings, and there was a general rush for the carriages. Nature abhors a acuum, even under the Naga Hills, and at the pioneer coal mines of Assam. It was half-past two; we had spent half an hour like five minutes in these wonderful collieries. But still lunch was a great and interesting fact, and it was at Margherita, with a lot to be done before we could get at it.

The train started back at 2-50 P.M. and reached Margherita at 3-15. Just as we ran in we exploded a series of fog-signals placed on the line, thus giving a sort of salute to the first coal train, which had shortly before passed over the Dehing bridge, and then started on its way to Dibrugarh.

The civilian European population of the train climbed its way up to the bungalow of Chevalier R. Paganini to collect itself for coming events; the martial element fell in to the sound of the bugle, and the natives dispersed to seek refreshment and repose.

Presently, from the verandah of Chevalier Paganini's hospitable bungalow, apparently elastic, from the numbers it accommodated *pro tem*, the sound of martial music was heard, and, headed by the band of the 42nd A.L.I., the Lakhimpur Volunteers marched up the road, turned the bungalow, and deployed at the back on some rather uneven ground, calculated to test the steadiness of that gallant corps on its legs in its subsequent manœuvres. Tree stumps and earth-work excavations are capital skirmishing cover, but a "march past" over such ground is somewhat trying. There were a large number of the hill-men present to see the *tamasha*, and it was amusing to see how they scattered and ran as the volunteers, headed by the band blaring forth martial music, appeared on the bungalow plateau. They gradually re-collected as they realised that no one was killed.

Major Beauclerk, in command, reported the arrival of the detachment of volunteers, and the Chief Commissioner, with Messrs. Ward, Murray and Geidt and Major Williams, took their stand on a rising ground, while the volunteers executed a march past, which was very creditable and steady under the circumstances. They then formed up again and fired a *feu de joie*, which caused another scattering of the tribes—Nagas, Singphos and Khamptis vieing with each other in their rush for the jungle. Three hearty cheers were then given, the Chief Commissioner said a few words of commendation to Major Beauclerk, and the volunteers were then marched up to the tiffin shed by Captain Kirwan, opposite to which they again piled arms and awaited the signal for an attack on the viands.

The rest of us were pretty hollow, too, by this time, and gladly hailed the move made by Mr. Elliot as he escorted Mrs. Beauclerk to the table. The ladies paired off rapidly and then there was a general rush by the crowd craving to fill the void.

The commissariat arrangements were in the hands of the Planters' Stores and Agency Company, and it was probably no easy task to feed a hungry multitude in the Naga Hills. The tiffin was very good indeed, but there was a lack of attendance, partly due to a notice given that no one was to take servants, to prevent overcrowding of natives in the train. The staff of servants taken by the caterers was rather inadequate to the demand, but there was plenty to eat and everything good, only people had to forage for themselves a good deal. The liquor was undeniable, Heidseck's dry Monopole being the staple

It was amusing to hear sundry comments made on this brand at one of the tables occupied by some of the miners and platelayers. "This aint much of a tipple, Bill" says a connoisseur. "Doan't know, 'Arry," replied one honest man; "Doan't know as I ever tasted none afore." But the connoisseur held to his point, and argued stoutly that "it wern t nought o' Champagne like as a could get at hoam."

It was past four o' clock before the volunteer review was over and we sat down to tiffiin. It took some time to satisfy the inner man when nearly 250 people had to be served, and it was getting on for five o'clock (although the programme laid down that we were to leave Margherita at three) before Mr. Benjamin Piercy rose from his seat and commenced his inaugurative speech, preliminary to the official declaration by the Chief Commissioner that the coal industry of Assam was open. The speeches took a long time, especially Mr. Piercy's, who orated at great length.

The Chief Commissioner declared the coal mines open, and Mr. J. Berry White also had a good deal to say.

Mr. White's speech was received with considerable applause, especially the end of it, and a general move was at once made for the train, the carriages meanwhile having been pushed across the Dehing bridge and the engine attached. The said engine was now whistling appealingly to us to hurry up. It was 5-30 P.M. before the speeches were over, and, owing to the irresistible tendency of an excursion crowd to straggle and take things easily till the very last moment, and then rush frantically over each other to their places, it was 6 P.M. before we were fairly off. As the Chief Commissioner had interjectionably noted in his speech, there were no lamps in the carriages, so we steamed along through the heart of the primeval forest—only a year or two back an impenetrable jungle haunted by wild and savage beasts, and as wild and savage men—in the blackness of darkness, illumined only by the red gleam in front from the engine lamps. The scene was occasionally lit up by the reflection on the smoke of the funnel from the open fire-box while stoking, but the momentary glare only served to intensify the blackness of the forest, bringing out tree trunks here and there into startling and ghostly relief against it as we glided past. At Bor bhil, where we stopped to water, and at the other bridges, where we slowed down to cross safely, strange yells, screams, barks and howlings broke out on the stillness of the night air, and at first made a few of the nervous start, thinking of wild animals. But most of us only smiled at first and swore *sotto voce* after-a-while as the clamour broke out again and again, whenever the lessening noise of the train going slow gave it a chance. We seemed to have the contents of Wombwell's menagerie or Noah's ark on board the train, but it was only some festive members in the rear carriages amusing themselves in their usual artless and childlike fashion *pour passer le temps.* Presently we get music instead—a decided improvement on the menagerie-business, and went marching through Georgia, a hunting to-day, after John Brown's body, over the garden wall, through the Makum forests in grand style, till we reached the junction at nine o'clock. Here there was another scramble for refreshments—biscuits and bottles of whisky, sandwiches and simpkin, coffee and claret were distributed as best they could be in the confusion. The lamps were put into the carriages, but nearly all shortly went out again, not being accustomed to their work evidently. The rest of the journey to Rehabari is a confused memory of snatches of sleep in cramped positions, occasional stoppages to drop passengers at various stations and points on the line, and an ever present faint sense of wonder as to where we were, and at what time would we get to Rehabari. The exertions of one gentleman, the General Manager for the Company, Mr. Hill, that night, deserve grateful mention. During the whole of this nightmare-like journey, back from Margherita to Rehabari, though he must have felt quite as tired and sleepy, and generally cross as most of us did, he was almost ubiquitous. At every stoppage he was up and down the whole length of the train, slipping placidly about in the mud, lantern in hand, good naturedly receiving chaff from the festive, and answering aggravating questions from the tired and grumpy; shouting out the name of the stopping place to arouse the attention of the drowsy who ought to get out there, then helping them out, seeing them to their conveyances, if of the gentler sex, and bidding them a cheery good-night. Most of us can be jolly under favourable circumstances, but Mr. Hill's task on that return journey from Margherita would have done credit to Mark Tapley's powers of "coming out strong." But we reached Rehabari at last at midnight. A long drive through the mud, and dinner, which was not over till 2 A.M., concluded the day for me, personally. And thinking of the Margherita tiffin (really our breakfast) hour, and our dinner, I went to bed feeling as if I were a real genuine "snark," one of whose chief peculiarities was, you remember, that "It always had breakfast at five o' clock tea, and dined on the following day."

The dinner by the Assam Railway Company to the Chief Commissioner, on the evening of the 19th instant, took place down at the "workshops," and was given in the engine-shed—a large corrugated iron roofed building, into which the engines retire for the night on ordinary occasions. For this special occasion, however, the engines had been relegated to outer darkness, the floor had been neatly planked down over the rails, with a floor-cloth covering the planks, and a cloth ceiling stretched overhead. The walls were draped with cloth and flags, while over the entrance, "Success to our enterprise" and at the opposite or ladies' retiring room end "Success to Makum coal" were inscribed in large letters. Altogether, taking into consideration the resources of the place and time available, the engine house was transformed into a very fine dining saloon. Our way was down by train from the Rehabari station,—

the train, by the way, timed to leave at 6-30 P.M. (the dinner was fixed for the early hour of 7 P.M.), really leaving, with the Dibrugarh punctuality, about 7-30. As we neared the workshops the scene was illuminated by a row of lamps along the line, and a number of huge fires of the veritable Makum coal, blazing merrily in the night, lighting up and absolutely warming the place all round, and making the advent of those who rode or drove down the road a little safer than it would otherwise have been.

Of the dinner itself perhaps the least said the better, and yet it is only fair to add that the resources of the caterers were severely taxed by the bulk of their material in the shape of crockery, etc., and the most of their men not having returned from the Margherita tiffin till noon of the next day, *i.e.*, the day of the dinner. We have not the Great Eastern Hotel, Messrs. Broad and McKinnel, or any of those skilled and well-stocked satisfiers of the inner man, to fall back on here, worse luck; and there are, doubtless, many excuses to be made for what must be characterised as a distinct failure in the way of dinner. It is one consolation to think that there was really plenty to eat provided before hand, and that what we did not get by reason of its not being cooked in time to serve up, went towards giving the British workmen next day an extremely "square meal."

The *menu* card, a prettily decorated one, with a Grecian or Roman maiden bringing in a tray of fruit, and a jar of something to drink—perhaps old Falernian —on the reverse, was somewhat curious in its nomenclature of the viands. Some of us tried to study out the peculiar applicability of the "nominations," but failed to penetrate the hidden mystery, or could not hit on the key. The *menu* is worth transcribing, though some knowledge of local places and personages is necessary to a full grasp of its scope.

POTAGES.

"Clear Oxtail" à la Bayley. Potage à la Crême.

POISSONS.

Saumon à l' Imperatrice Glacé de Mahseer, à la Indes des Dehing.

ENTREES.

Volauvents à la Elliott. Cotelets glacées de Marcheviel.

Gratin de Pigeons à la Paganini.

PIÉCES DE RESISTENCE.

Dindon rôtis (truffles) à la Panitola. Boeuf Boulli à la Hill.

Selle de Mouton à la Lakhimpur Rifle Corps.

Jambons garnis à la Sprenger.

HORS DŒUVRES.

Asperges à la Ward. Pate de Foie grás á la Beauclerk.

Champignons Sartines à la Piercy.

ENTREMETS.

Blance Mange à "Tipsy Pudding" de la Berry White de Makum

Jelly Vanille à la Margherita. Mince pies de Thikak ; Gateaux divers de Ledo.

Desserts, Comfitures, etc, à la Godfrey.

The *menu* is certainly curious. So was the dinner unique. They fitted.

"THE PLANTER."

THE misconceptions as to the planter, his ways, habits and tastes, have been many and various. The "brutal planter;" *Messieurs les 'planters' du thé, les sauvages*; the wild European tribes on the North-East frontier—these are a few of the pet names which have been bestowed, half in jest, and half in earnest, on the men who are rapidly transforming by their capital and energy what was a wild, almost unknown tract of jungle, into one of the most flourishing and promising provinces of the Indian Empire. But it is gradually becoming acknowledged that the transferring of a man from the civilising and softening influences of home life, does not necessarily brutalise him. It is now recognised that education and refinement are not utterly lost and forgotten as a result of engaging in the management of a tea garden; that men who are gentle, kind and forbearing, do not become savages in habits and manners when they "go into tea." The planter whose chief enjoyment is torturing his coolies, and who spends all his leisure in thinking out new places to hit them on, where they cannot by any freak of nature wear those fragile articles, their spleens, exists now only in some of the lower vernacular papers. There may be a hazy shadow of that ideal planter still lingering in such official minds as have not cast off the trammels of the old belief, that all outside the magic circle of red tape and "the services" were necessarily *canaille*—brutes, dead to all the higher and nobler feelings and aspirations of weak human nature. But even by official minds it is now generally admitted that planters also are God's creatures—men with natures and passions even like unto themselves.

With a view to satisfy our own and non-planting reader's curiosity on the subject of the planter's nature and habits, we have recently sent a special commissioner to study the *genus* in his native wilds. Indigo planters are an older and better known species—their *habitat* has been exploited and their peculiarities noted often. Our enquiries have been particularly directed to the tea-planter *Assamiensis*.

The Assam planter may be divided, generally, into four classes as to original derivation—the young man with a little capital, who comes out to learn tea-planting with a view to investing, or to making a garden of his own ; the "tea expert," or Mincing Lane young man, who comes out to show the old hands how to make tea, and finds he has a great deal to learn (and unlearn) himself in the process ; the youth who has sisters, cousins, or aunts, on the board of direction of some big flourishing company, and who comes out to a sort of "covenanted" birth, and sails serenely on to shares and success, unless he happens to turn out a particularly bad egg. The "practical engineer", who came in with the development of tea machinery, to look after the engine and its adjuncts, and who often developes into a thoroughly practical tea-planter all round. There is a fifth class, also practical, the "practical gardener"—commonly known as the "P.G." He also occasionally developes," into a thoroughly good practical "all round" man, but generally on the Darwinian principle of "the survival of the fittest." Experience on tea gardens has taught most owners and agents that the course of the P.G. to success and a big management bears out the Scriptual dictum, "Many are called, but few are chosen."

Making allowances for the differences of home training and education, and for the individual idiosyncracies of human beings, tea planters are very much alike and very like other men, too.

Some of them are married, some are not, and some are absolutely bachelors. Some of them always dress for dinner; some dine (in the hot weather) in a pair of unmentionables and a singlet. But they all "tub," which is one thing in their favour. Some of them drink claret, hock, and champagne; most of them have a discriminating taste in whiskies; beer is a very common beverage also. A few—a *very* few—are teetotal. They all eat fowl, however, because they very often can get nothing else to eat. Some of them get angry when stupid people annoy them, and swear, and occasionally even hit the stupid people. But careful enquiry has led us to believe that other Europeans in India do so too—men in the "services," members of the bar, august personages on the bench, even editors, occasionally are tempted this way and fall. Anger is a passion common to humanity.

Englishmen—or Britishers (which covers the

ground better)—are sadly prone to hit from the shoulder on provocation. Our Aryan brother prefers to allude to his enemies' female relatives, even unto the third and fourth generation. This is one of the points wherein we differ from our Aryan brethren.

One view of the planter's life, lately current, was that he spent his time chiefly at polo, race meets and training garden ponies. Because thou art virtuous, oh, Calcutta agent! and confinest thyself to thy desk, if thy seat on a "gee" is not adhesive enough to stand paperchases out Ballygunge way, shall the poor planter be debarred from cakes and ale once in six months? Because he gets up a race meet at Dibrugarh, Sibsaugor or Tezpur once a year, has the planter therefore no ceaseless toil, no daily round, "no clod-hopping" over clearances, no deep hoeing to tramp round, no daily wettings through in the rains, as he goes round his "plucking," no days of parboiling in the tea-house, from morn to extremely dewy eve, in a temperature of about 120°? And above all, has he no "scorchers" in the way of correspondence from agents or directors to cogitate over and reply to, when mind and body are alike depressed by enervating toil, and temper enervated by weather, machinery going wrong, coolies bolting, fever lurking in the system, and fellows writing "Sketches in Assam." "Go to"! saith the planter; "Go to"—anywhere you like, but go in the assurance that "the planter's life is not a happy one."

Indeed his woes and miseries are sometimes as heavy and varied as Job's were, and he cannot scrape any of them off with a potsherd as the patriarch did. In addition to the work and worries above alluded to, which are perhaps only his share—a larger sized one—of the primeval curse, the planter has some special troubles peculiar to himself. It does not usually fall to the lot of other men to be dismissed sometimes by telegram, and often merely by a letter asking him to dâk out and hand over charge to his successor because he has done his duty to his owners and "nursed up" an overworked garden, expended too much money on necessary cultivation or buildings, or has been afflicted by Providence with bad weather or blight. This is a special treat reserved for planters. The *kacherri* and its myrmidons mark the planter as their special prey. Grog-shops are put at his door to poison his imported labour. But the climax is the returns the planter is called on to fill up and send in. If there is one thing the average planter hates more than another, it is writing. The sight of a pen, ink and paper his soul abhors. Figures are an abomination to him—statistical ones particularly. Yet our paternal Government showers form after form, each having a more bewildering array of columns than the last, upon his devoted head; and promptly fines him, or sends body warrants after him, if the said forms are not punctually filled in and returned at due date. Government knows his weakness, and nobly educates him out of it. It is only through trial and suffering that perfection comes. Government seeks to evolve the perfect planter.

But there is a silver lining to every cloud. The *Gazette* (official) occasionally publishes "Resolutions" in which the chief local torturer gets "slated" for the incorrectness, incompleteness, or arrears of tea returns from his district. The planter reads these. He realises that others are suffering for his shortcomings, and rejoicing exclaims, "*Chokra ! áru etta* "*peg*" *daibè dé !*" And he meets the D.C. at polo or tennis shortly afterwards, and asks him guilelessly if he has seen the C. C's latest sarcasm, and his soul is filled with great peace as the D. C. scowls at him.

"Toiling, rejoicing, sorrowing," the planter works on from day to day ; dispensing freehanded hospitality to all and sundry who pass his bungalow, and looking forward more or less hopefully to a rest—even if temporary—from his labours and a trip home, where agents trouble not, and where coolie returns and red spider are alike at rest.

"THE RIVER."

To the Assamese there is only one river. But as out-siders are taught, in their geography days at school, of other rivers, it is perhaps better to specify our creed. There is no river but the Brahmaputra, and the steamer captains are its prophets. They used to net its profits too, in days gone by. This remark *sotto voce*, in small type please, or it might hurt their feelings, saddened and soured by the memories of other days, when freight and commissions were high, and planter-passengers numerous and festive. But now we seldom go purely and simply "on the river" as we used to. If we are on business we hurry-down and up again by the mail. If we are seedy, we likewise, generally go by mail, to get a change somewhere :—up to the hills, down to Ceylon, or—blessed hope—perhaps home for six months. With Dibrugarh only twenty odd days from London, *viâ* Dhubri, Kannia, Bombay and Brindisi, a man can put in a wholesome month's dissipation and general cussedness in London, out of three months' leave even if he is tolerably energetic about it.

The patriarch Job once observed "Man is born to trouble as the sparks fly upwards." He was troubled with boils at the time and so off his usual serenity of mind, but he made a bull's-eye that shot nevertheless. We get boils in Assam too and liver, and whiskey, and other annoying things. I have been tempted to write a little alphabet of our grievances and respectfully commend it to the notice of parents and guardians of the rising generation who are about to "come out and go into tea." If we could only get Kate Greenaway to illustrate it, Walter Crane to set it to music, and Routledge to publish it, it might be called the Baby Planters' Opera.

A. Are the agents we all have to please.
B. Are the brokers who value our teas.
Cc. Sends us forms to fill up at our leisure.
D.—Is the word which expresses our pleasure.
E. Is our engine which always goes wrong.
F. Is the fever which comes on so strong.
G. Are the gharris whose wrecks strew the ground.
H. Is the hoeing we have to trudge round.
I. Is flammation attacking our liver.
J. Is the journey we take up the river.
K. Is the *Kyah* with such a long bill.
L. Is the license at grog-shops to swill.
M. Is the mouzadar coming for rent.
N. Is the number of dibs we have spent.
O. Are the oaths which we—some of us—use
at P. The poor prices we read in the news.
Q. Quarrelsome neighbours who *phûsilau* coolies.
R. The red spider that ruins our *pùlis*.
S. Is the "sack" at the end of the season.
T. Is the tipling, that's (sometimes) the reason.
U. Our queer uniforms, volunteer pageant.
V. That infliction, the "visiting agent."
W. The whiskey we—some of us—drink.
X. Is "ex-dividend," *nil*, I should think.

Y. Is the young man who goes on the spree.

Z. Are the "zanies" who "go into tea."

The alphabet is exhausted, but our troubles and grievances are by no means used up. Feeble from fever, bothered by boils, agitated by agents, cramped by Calcutta charges, anxious over gloomy anticipations of short crop, poor prices, and the inevitable *taili*, *bostu*, *bora*, or "sack" at the end of the season, we are going to take a "run on the river."

One does not take a run on the river in the present advanced stage of Assamese civilisation for pleasure. Nor as before noted on business. A few who cannot get leave enough for a trip to Shillong, to Darjeeling, out to sea, or home, when "hipped" or generally "below par", take a run down by one steamer and up by another purely for health's sake In this case, with nothing to do, and lots of time to do it in, the state of the tongue, the colour of the so-called "whites" of the eyes, and various other facial indications, require study. The looking-glass, which is generally found screwed against the bulk-head of one's cabin, becomes a confidential friend and adviser; it is much more interesting than the scenery on the banks, and opens out a wider field for speculation.

The cabin itself is such a change—for the better—from the patent canvas shower-baths these steamers used to try and delude the public into the belief they had cabin accommodation with! I once sat up in bed all night in one of these steamers with a waterproof sheet and umbrella over me and my wife, and then when I complained about it, a perfect stranger came and "took my scalp" with all the freedom of an old acquaintance! Now, there is a water-proof, taut-stretched roof on a substantial framework overhead; and the cabins themselves are larger and more comfortable than those on the big steamers. The food question is still uncertain, according to the idiosyncracy of the individual *khansamah*, but as a rule it is much better than it used to be. There is a want of originality about the *menu* certainly. Mail steamer Hindustani for *tiffin* means sardines, cheese rind, and that sort of carriage wheel grease they think is butter. Although these boats run as regularly as trains, touching at large stations within certain fixed hours, the *khansamahs* never seem able to arrange for fresh bread, milk, or vegetables. And why is man a nocturnal animal to a certain extent, condemned to go to bed with the sun, or sit in the dark? The wretched old-fashioned ship's lantern only makes darkness dimly visible; and the as old-fashioned candles never have shades, so the dips blow out if you wink at them. If the company would sell or pawn those huge useless plated jugs, too big and heavy to handle freely as drinking jugs and yet too small to bathe in, and invest the proceeds in stormproof "meteor" lamps from Theodore Knaust, they would save a lot on profanity of the part of the passengers. There are four new mail boats on the river now—larger vessels, upperdecked over all, and very fast boats. But as the cabins are modelled on a very old-fashioned ship's cabin, small, confined, and stuffy with wretched little bunks, and are on the lower deck,; and as the upper deck is given up to coolies, most of us prefer the older and smaller boats for comfort. But the new mail boats have their advantages. They go well and seem to be gymnasts in good training. The *serang* charges sand-banks at full speed and generally gets over with a jump. The sensation is curious at first, and the shock unpleasant. But after you have been turned inside out once or twice, you get used to it.

Anchored—or rather moored at some station for the night—one generally meets some steamer folk and hears a lot of river talk. With eight or ten new steamers belonging to the old companies, and the fine boats of the Inland Flotilla Company, the river is getting crowded. The talk is of freights, invasion of vested interests, and laments over lost commission. Competition is keen. Enthusiastic skippers of the old lines discuss the division of the spoil when they have busted the Inland Flotilla Company and run them off the river.* The India General Steam Navigation will take over two steamers and half a dozen flats; the Rivers Steam Navigation Company, ditto. These gentlemen forget the fate of the old girl who counted her chickens before they were hatched. Meanwhile tariff rates are nowhere, shares decline merrily, and the wily *kyah* waxes fat and rejoices at getting his freight carried free, with a percentage on shipments to encourage him. The Brahmaputra Steam Companies are rapidly approaching the condition of the rival Colonial lines—New Zealand, I think. One company advertised freight free. The other promptly replied by carrying shippers free also. Number one

* Which was done in a year!

retorted by throwing in free mess and liquor. Number two scored again by offering return tickets on the same terms, and threw in shore expenses, including hotel bills and a free pass to the theatres and concerts at temporary destination between trips. They both smashed of course, and a new company picked up the pieces. *Verbum sapienti* fix a moderate reasonable rate for passengers and *stick to it.*

How soon one who travels much on the river picks up river talk. In a few trips up and down, one gets to know, either personally or by reputation, all hands pretty nearly. Like the rest of the world, steamer folk are somewhat mixed. It takes all sorts of people to make a world, even a little world like the Brahmaputra one. There is a great deal of human nature in man wherever you meet him. The river has collected all sorts of "characters," from the old Fathers of the Brahmaputra Flotilla—few of whom are now afloat—down to the "silent member," and still newer-fledged skippers. To a man who has nothing better to do, the river affords a fine field for the study of character; while the stories one hears are as various as the people who tell them. From grave to gay—tragedy, comedy and farce, all have their share. One hears of deaths—some of them of tragic nature and under heartrending circumstances, that the waters of the river have caused; of marriages that have been "instigated" on its placid waters; of flirtations which—some of them—ought to have ended in marriage, but did not. There are sprees on record of all sorts and sizes, from the "drunk" of the mate and the engineers, up to the more pretentious "larks" of the aristocratic cabin passengers, both alike a curious mixture of alcoholic stimulants, cards and so-called "weaker vessels" and human "cussedness" generally. All these sayings and doings still await their mundane recording angel. The Brahmaputra sighs for its historian. With the gigantic strides made within the last few years in "improving communications," the old traditions of the river are fast dying out. New steamers crowd the river, new men, new *dastûr* are in the ascendent; there are few of the old hands left now. New kings have arisen who know not Joseph—nor any of his brethren; the old order of things passeth away.

But he would be a bold man who should attempt to do for the Brahmaputra and its steamer life, what Mark Twain has done for the other big steamer-haunted river of the world, in his "Life on the Mississipi." And yet what an interesting volume it would make! But I would like to secure a passage to some far distant country where I could live disguised, unknown and unrecognised, and start the day before the book was published. No sane Insurance Company would accept a policy. Will no one step in and take the laurels and scalping, awaiting the historian of the Brahmaputra? A series of "queer stories" imbedded in *Truth*, would make his fortune and make a number of readers very anxious to attend his funeral. I would like to try it myself, but I have not hair enough left to grace the wigwams of those who would promptly dig up the tomahawk and sally forth on the war-path. For the "Records of the River," the fitting hour has arrived. But where is the man?